READING
WRITING
AND
LITERACY 2.0

READING
WRITING
AND
LITERACY 2.0

Teaching with Online Texts, Tools, and Resources, K–8

Denise Johnson

Foreword by Donald J. Leu

Teachers College, Columbia University
New York and London

International Reading Association
Newark, DE

Published by Teachers College Press, 1234 Amsterdam Avenue, New York, NY 10027

Library of Congress Cataloging-in-Publication Data

Johnson, Denise.
Reading, writing, and literacy 2.0 : teaching with online texts, tools, and resources, K–8 / Denise Johnson.
   pages cm
Includes bibliographical references and index.
ISBN 978-0-8077-5529-7 (pbk. : alk. paper)
ISBN 978-0-8077-7285-0 (ebook)
   1. Language arts—Computer network resources. 2. Computers and literacy. I. Title.
LB1576.7.J64 2014
372.60285 2 23   2013046364

ISBN 978-0-8077-5529-7 (paper)
eISBN 978-0-8077-7285-0 (ebook)

Printed on acid-free paper
Manufactured in the United States of America

21 20 19 18 17 16 15 14   8 7 6 5 4 3 2 1

Contents

Foreword

Benjy was one of my favorite students. There was something about Benjy that was very predictable. Each time he came back from the library with a new book, my class and I knew we would soon hear his excited voice over the hum of other important work that was taking place. "Oh, boy, oh, boy!" would come floating through the air as he sat down to read his new treasure. We always smiled and then went back to our work.

This memory came to me as I was reading Denise Johnson's wonderful contribution, *Reading, Writing, and Literacy 2.0*. With each chapter, I found myself saying, "Oh, boy, oh, boy!" Smiling, I recalled my classroom and Benjy.

Here is an exceptional new book that will have a profound effect on teaching, making your work fresh and exciting while you prepare students for their future in an online age of information and communication. With the Internet and so many new technologies for literacy and learning appearing on a regular basis, the central role that we play in orchestrating literacy and learning experiences for our students will increase, not decrease. In addition, we will be challenged to thoughtfully guide their learning within information environments that are richer and more complex than traditional print media, presenting richer and more complex learning opportunities for both us and our students. *Reading, Writing, and Literacy 2.0* shows us how.

There are many things that I love about this book. It is written with a voice wise to both the opportunities and the challenges of classroom teaching. It also contains a vast number of ideas that can be immediately used in your classroom. Of course, too, it describes effective teaching of new literacies with so many new technologies. In addition, it begins by providing a clear and compelling framework to put all of the upcoming ideas into a package that will make perfect sense to any teacher.

Perhaps most importantly, though, this is not simply a book about technology for technology's sake. Between the covers you will discover new ideas about every single part of your literacy program: language development, building classroom community, connecting with families, vocabulary, fluency, literature, comprehension, writing, inquiry, assessment, and even your continuing professional development. In masterful fashion, Denise Johnson weaves powerful models of instruction and specific teaching ideas into each of these areas with the technologies that best supports each one. You come to understand that Denise is, straight up, a teacher's teacher. You will gain greatly from meeting her in these pages and learning what she has to say about the new literacies that define literacy today and defines the future our students will build with your help.

As you know, the Common Core State Standards is an important new initiative that impacts many classrooms in our nation. Three major changes are at the heart of these changes. First, there is an increased emphasis on higher-level thinking. Second, there is greater attention paid to informational text reading. And finally, the Internet and other technologies are integrated into instruction. This exceptional new contribution by Denise Johnson will provide us with needed support in all three areas. Oh, boy! Oh, boy!

—Donald J. Leu,
Neag Chair in Literacy and Technology
University of Connecticut, Neag School of Education

Preface

The shift from Web 1.0 to Web 2.0 engenders a whole new ethos or worldview that values and promotes participation, collaboration, and distribution (Lankshear & Knobel, 2006). The same ethos drives literacy 2.0. Reading, writing, listening, and speaking in the context of the Internet *is* participating, collaborating, and sharing distributed knowledge and expertise.

Knobel and Wilber (2009) believe "Literacy 2.0 is not simply an upgrade from literacy 1.0—it's truly a paradigm shift" (p. 23). It is this book's contention that classroom teachers are the foundation of this paradigm shift, as effective literacy instruction encompasses collaboration, participation, and sharing of knowledge. It is not the underlying philosophy teachers must embrace, but the medium. Shirky (2010) writes, "To understand what we can make of this new resource, we have to understand not just the kind of actions it makes possible but the hows and wheres of those actions" (pp. 27–28). With an understanding of the differences between traditional and online reading outlined in this book, classroom teachers are ready to take the next steps to the "hows and wheres" of effective instruction. By understanding the "hows and wheres" of online reading, writing, and communicating, teachers can scaffold children's engagement with digital environments to foster deep reading.

The way children learn to engage with digital environments today will impact their literacy future in important ways. Yet, Baker, Pearson, and Rozendal (2010) ask:

> [H]ow often do we see the literacy skills associated with reading and writing with communication technologies represented in our school curricula? If our schools continue to limit the literacy curriculum to reading and writing traditional, alphabetic, printed texts, then our children will be well prepared for 1950 but ill prepared for 2050. (p. 2)

Koehler and Mishra (2008) point out that curricula do not exist independently of teachers: "Teachers construct curricula through an organic process of iterative design and refinement, negotiating among existing constraints, to create contingent conditions for learning" (p. 21). Teachers construct and enact curriculum—teachers are *curriculum designers.*

The purpose of this book is to bridge the gap between the false dichotomy of either print *or* digital media, pedagogy *or* technology, 1950 *or* 2050. This book is intended to provide a framework to assist teachers in using their content and pedagogical expertise in flexible ways to create a literacy curriculum that includes the instruction of new literacies within digital environments. It is not intended to set forth a curriculum or serve as a manual but to provide examples of ways this might be done.

Chapter 1, "What Is Literacy 2.0 and What Happened to Literacy 1.0?" focuses on the shift that has occurred from the traditional analog definition of literacy and literacy teaching and learning. This chapter will define literacy 2.0 as the broad range of skills and strategies children of today will need to successfully live and work in the 21st century. These skills include the use of technology but also creativity and innovation, critical thinking and problem solving, communication, collaboration, flexibility and adaptability, initiation and self-direction, social and cross-cultural skills, and productivity and accountability. Educators must view literacy as a matter of engaging in the ever-developing process of using reading and writing as tools for thinking and learning in order to expand students' understanding of themselves and the world. The chapter will explain why classroom teachers are perfectly positioned to build and extend these skills and strategies within the literacy curriculum.

Chapter 2, "A Framework for Literacy 2.0 Thinking," presents a framework teachers can use to facilitate their understanding of how to integrate technology, pedagogy, and content knowledge in a meaningful way. The preparation and support children will need to meet the challenges of the 21st century will depend as much on *how* they are taught as *what* they are taught; in other words, the pedagogy of literacy instruction is just as important as the content of the literacy curriculum.

This chapter begins with a discussion of Technological Pedagogical Content Knowledge (TPACK) and how this framework can guide decisionmaking for effectively integrating technology into the literacy curriculum. NCTE's 21st Century Skills Framework will also be discussed as a way to think about planning, supporting, and assessing student learning. Finally, the chapter will present the Internet reciprocal teaching (IRT) instructional routine for creating effective lessons that support teaching the skills, strategies, and dispositions necessary for learning to effectively read, write, and communicate in digital environments.

IRT lessons are a key feature in Chapters 3–8. There is a lesson for younger students, primarily targeting grades K–3, and a lesson for older students, primarily targeting grades 4–8. However, teachers should adapt these lessons depending on their students' technological and content knowledge. Additionally, the types of computers and equipment used and the length of each phase of the lesson will also vary depending on available resources and scheduling. The online applications used throughout the book are free of charge and usually can be used across multiple platforms.

Chapter 3, "Creating Classroom Community and Connecting with Families," looks at ways to use technology to create classroom community and connect the classroom to the community and students' families.

Chapter 4, "Vocabulary and Fluency," discusses ways to integrate technology to promote word recognition, word study, vocabulary development and fluency

Chapter 5, "Sites and Selection Criteria for Ebooks," defines the categories and structures of e-texts and provides considerations for selecting quality, well-designed e-texts for students.

Chapter 6, "Using E-Tools to Scaffold Comprehension of E-Literature," examines the principles underlying the design of the digital environment and considers how to apply well-validated approaches to teaching comprehension with print materials before, during, and after reading.

Chapter 7, "Writing Online," demonstrates ways to integrate technology to promote the writing process and publishing through collaborative peer editing, the use of online images and photos, online publishing, creating digital storybooks, and more.

Chapter 8, "Technology Across the Curriculum," reflects how to integrate technology to promote content-area learning including the use of visual thinkmaps, online graphic organizers, online annotation and note-taking tools, Internet projects, and Internet inquiry.

Chapter 9, "Assessment in a Literacy 2.0 Environment," shows how technology applications can assist teachers in capturing the multiple dimensions of students' thinking and learning and can inform critical decisions about future instruction. In the technology applications discussed in Chapters 3–7, the students were engaged in authentic, creative, and often collaborative learning in which the technology was simply the tool that allowed for meaningful knowledge construction. This type of learning allows educators to assess students' crucial thinking about literacy in a way that more traditional forms of assessment could not.

Chapter 10, "What About Literacy 3.0? Continuing Professional Development," reviews the importance and challenge of staying current with the continual changes that are inevitable in our information society in order to continue to teach children in ways that will prepare and support them in meeting the challenges of the 21st century. A myriad of ways to stay abreast of research and technology tools is provided, including blogs, social networks, professional association resources, and videos/webinars.

The Literacy 2.0 Companion Blog (literacytwopointzero.blogspot.com) provides links to all of the resources discussed or listed throughout this book. If any of the links change, they will be updated on the site. Additional resources to support the use of tools or to highlight teaching practices utilizing these tools will also be included. Regular posts will highlight new online resources that enhance literacy learning and ways literacy teachers are using technology in their classrooms. If you have resources, strategies, or stories you would like to share, please send them through the contact information on the blog.

CHAPTER 1

What Is Literacy 2.0 and What Happened to Literacy 1.0?

In the fictional story *Whittington* (2005) by Alan Armstrong, the roughneck tomcat Whittington arrives one day at a barn where he gradually befriends a ragtag group of animals rescued by the barn's owner, Bernie. When the year's first big snowstorm traps the animals in the barn, Whittington begins telling the story of his namesake, Dick Whittington, to an audience that includes the animals and grows to include Bernie's orphaned grandchildren, Ben and Abby. The feline continues the story as winter grinds on, and the children and animals absorb Dick's tale of hard work and struggles, which parallels that of 8-year-old Ben, who is having trouble learning to read. At one point in the story, Bernie receives a letter from Ben's school:

> The letter said that Ben wasn't reading up to grade level and there were problems with his temper. Sometimes when asked to read, he'd throw the book down. He was classified as an "At Risk" student—at risk of failing because of his poor reading. (p. 104)

Later, Ben meets his new reading teacher,

> "I'm Miss O'Brian," said the teacher, turning to Ben and putting out her hand. "The kids call me Coach O." Her hand was small and cool. She had a soft voice. "Let's spend a minute reading together before you go back to your room. How about reading me this?"
> Ben did his best. His reading was ragged. She helped him along, smiling, nodding, making notes. "Good," she said after a few minutes. "I think I know what's going on. I can help you." (pp. 131–132)

This is an unforgettable tale about the healing, transcendent power of storytelling, and how learning to read saves one little boy. Literacy changes the way children see themselves—as readers—as members of a different group. Literacy opens the door to the world and has the power to change lives.

ONLINE READING: A LITERACY ISSUE

It happens that Coach O is a Reading Recovery teacher. She has spent a great deal of time ascertaining the critical qualities of knowledge and practice needed to offer outstanding literacy instruction to beginning readers. Reading Recovery teachers, like all excellent teachers of reading, have an in-depth knowledge of the cognitive, social, and emotional aspects of how children learn to read. As Coach O observed Ben's reading behaviors, she took notes—possibly a running record—that captured how he processed information, monitored his understanding, problem solved and self-corrected while reading. This information, collected and analyzed over time, will assist Coach O in using what she knows about the reading process, as compared to what she has observed in Ben's reading behavior, to determine an instructional plan to help him become an effective reader. This includes asking Ben to read text and use strategies that are within his zone of proximal development so that he will not become frustrated and angry.

According to the International Reading Association's (IRA) 2000 position statement *Excellent Reading Teachers,* such teachers:

- understand reading and writing development
- continually assess children's individual progress and relate reading instruction to children's previous experiences
- know a variety of ways to teach reading
- offer a variety of materials and texts for children to read
- use flexible grouping strategies
- are good reading "coaches"

In addition, excellent reading teachers have strong content and pedagogical knowledge, manage classrooms so that there is a high rate of engagement, use strong motivational strategies that encourage independent learning, have high expectations for children's achievement, and help children who are having difficulty (IRA, 2000, p. 1). From this list of distinguishing qualities of knowledge and practice, it is easy to see why excellent reading teachers make a difference in children's reading achievement and motivation to read.

However, if Ben were starting 1st grade this fall, he would graduate in 2025. What do you predict about the world in which he will live and work? I'm sure your response has something to do with the proliferation and influence of technology. According to Shirky (2010):

> In 2010 the global internet-connected population will cross two billion people, and mobile phone accounts already number over three billion. Since there are something like 4.5 billion adults worldwide (roughly 30 percent of the global population is under fifteen), we live, for the first time in history, in a world where being part of a globally interconnected group is the normal case for most citizens. (pp. 23–24)

There is much debate in U.S. society around book reading versus Internet reading, prompted by headlines such as "Is Google Making Us Stupid?" and "Online Literacy Is a Lesser Kind." Yet, with the staggering statistics of current and predicted Internet access, online reading is not an either-or proposition. Sixty-five percent of U.S. adults have high-speed broadband Internet connections at home and 93% have a cell phone (Pew Internet, 2013).

What will it mean to be literate in the 3rd decade of the 21st century? In an online survey conducted by the Pew Research Center (Anderson & Rainie, 2010), 895 technology stakeholders and critics were asked about their expectations of social, political, and economic change by 2020. One question asked respondents to predict the Internet's influence on the future of knowledge-sharing in 2020, specifically what would likely stay the same or be different when it comes to reading and writing and other displays of information, and what would be the future of books. The following quotes exemplify two recurring themes in the respondents' answers:

> Reading and writing will be different in 10 years. Language has always evolved to embrace new realities and it is evolving now. There will be a new fluidity in media creation. Visual representations and storytelling will be important in new ways, so "screen" literacy will emerge. (p. 26)

> The nature of writing has changed now, especially since so much of it takes place in public. The quality of the new material will get better over time, in part because these new social media creators will get feedback and learn. Today's changes parallel other historic changes that occurred when new technologies came on the scene. (p. 28)

When asked if this change would be positive or negative, 65% of the expert respondents agreed that "by 2020 it will be clear that the Internet has enhanced and improved reading, writing and the rendering of knowledge" (Anderson & Rainie, 2010, p. 3). Yet the 2000 IRA position statement on excellent reading teachers focuses solely on traditional printed text with no mention of computers, digital text, Internet communication technologies (ICTs), or mobile technology of any kind. Not to undervalue the importance of the foundational literacies required to read traditional print, but it is clear that "literacy is no longer a static construct; it has now come to mean a rapid and continuous process of change in the ways in which we read, write, view, listen, compose, and communicate information" (Coiro, Knobel, Lankshear, & Leu, 2008, p. 5). In other words, the acquisition of new literacies requires traditional as well as new reading, writing, and communicating skills.

Effective reading instruction is also dependent on teachers' beliefs. The way teachers think about, understand, and value literacy instruction influences their practice (Tschannen-Moran & Johnson, 2011). Whether Ben and his counterparts around the world merely survive or positively thrive in the decades to come depends in large measure on the experiences they have in school, especially with classroom teachers who are uniquely qualified to prepare them for their literacy futures. As Leu (2006) states, "The Internet is a reading and literacy issue, not a technology issue" (p. 6). If classroom teachers see the Internet as a context in which to read, write, and communicate, then it is no more a technology than is a book; that is, "its functional affordances define it more than its technological affordances" (Leu, O'Byrne, Zawilinski, McVerry, & Everett-Cacopardo, 2009, p. 265). In this case, the medium is *not* the message—the medium is just the medium. The foundational premise of this book is that classroom teachers are perfectly positioned to build and extend the new literacies of the Internet within the literacy curriculum, since "New literacies will be required to function in this world. In fact, the Internet might change the very notion of what it means to be smart" (Anderson & Rainie, 2010, p. 19).

THE NEW LITERACIES OF READING, WRITING, AND COMMUNICATING

New literacies (also known as 21st-century literacies, Internet literacies, digital literacies, new media literacies, multiliteracies, information literacy, ICT literacies, and computer literacy) is an umbrella term that has emerged to encompass the vast range of multidisciplinary research to define the

> skills, strategies, and dispositions necessary to successfully use and adapt to the rapidly changing information and communication technologies and contexts that continuously emerge in our world and influence all areas of our personal and professional lives. (Leu, Kinzer, Coiro, & Cammack, 2004, p. 1572)

The skills involve creativity, communication, collaboration, critical thinking, and comprehension. The acquisition of these skills requires the use of strategies to identify important questions, locate relevant information, and crucially evaluate, synthesize, and communicate information from the Internet and other ICTs to others. Certain dispositions such as persistence, flexibility, collaboration, critical stance, and reflection are necessary to engage with information in a thoughtful and meaningful way (Coiro, 2012).

Children today are digital natives (also called Generation Y, Millennial Generation, Generation Next, or Net Generation). Ninety-three percent of children ages 8–18 spend an average of 90 minutes a day using their home computers (Kaiser Foundation, 2010). Almost 75% of this time is spent on social networking, instant messaging, watching videos, and playing computer games. Even very young children come to school having either firsthand experience or experience with their parents' or siblings' email, cell phones, iPods, and digital cameras. Although many children come to school already familiar with digital media, they do not know how to fully access and engage with them. Most students use the Internet to extend friendships or entertain themselves, but only a small percentage of children use the Internet to explore their interests or find information beyond what they have access to at school or in their community (Ito et al., 2008; Kaiser Foundation, 2010). *The difference may be in the way children think about themselves while engaged.* Children know the Internet keeps people well informed, but informed about what? Trends? Current issues? Pop culture? The lack of engagement with the Internet as a learning resource suggests new ways of thinking about the role of classroom teachers.

As demonstrated by Coach O, teachers have acquired an in-depth knowledge of the content and pedagogy required to support children in learning to read traditional print. To prepare children to read, write, and communicate in digital environments, however, teachers must understand the affordances and constraints of this new context.

In other words, what is the same and what is different or "new" about reading, writing, and communicating online? The sections that follow on reading, writing, communicating, and social context provide as much information as is currently available on what is the same and what is different in online reading contexts.

Reading

The RAND Study Group (2002) defines comprehension as "the process of simultaneously extracting and constructing meaning through interaction and involvement with written language" (p. 12). Reading comprehension consists of three elements: the reader, the text, and the activity of reading. The unique exchange among the reader, the text, and the activity occurs within a larger sociocultural context that shapes and is shaped by the reader. Some researchers (Coiro, 2003; Coiro & Dobler, 2007; Kymes, 2005; Leu, Kinzer, Coiro, & Cammack, 2004) have argued that conventional understandings of these three elements are not always sufficient for understanding reading comprehension in electronic and networked information environments. Research and practice in these three areas may provide some insight.

The Text

The features of any written text have a large impact on how the reader constructs representations of the text and comprehends text. According to the RAND Study Group (2002), those representations embedded in the text include:

- surface code (the exact wording of the text)
- text base (idea units representing the meaning of the text)
- mental models (the way in which information is processed for meaning)

The RAND Study Group (2002) acknowledges that

> Electronic text presents particular challenges to comprehension (e.g., dealing with the non-linear nature of hypertext), but it also offers the potential to support comprehension by providing hyperlinks to definitions of unknown words or other supplementary material. (p. xv)

As described in the following sections, these challenges and support are an inherent part of the structure or genre of digital environments and whether the digital environment is open or closed.

Digital Text as Genre. When children begin to read traditional printed text, they usually do so with at least a basic understanding of how stories work—concepts about print (text is read from left to right and top to bottom, pages are turned left to right, print carries meaning, etc.) and story structure, or genre (fiction and nonfiction). Genre, an often overlooked cueing system in reading, constrains readers' predictions and lays a path for reading (Bomer, 1995). Each genre is unique and requires certain strategies for reading, so it is not safe to assume that students who are competent in one genre will have no problem mastering others. Studies have shown that primary-age children are typically less exposed to information text than narrative text and therefore have more difficulty reading it (Duke, 2000).

To fully understand the difference in the literacy demands on the reader, it is important to understand that the structure, or genre, of digital text is different from printed text. The interactive structure of digital texts distinguishes them from other genres. Therefore, it is important for children to understand the concept and structure of digital text before they attempt to make meaning from it. Table 1.1 summarizes the main differences between traditional print and digital environments.

Open and Closed Networked Environments. A closed environment refers to a static system that is self-contained; that is, only certain content is available. Examples of

Table 1.1. Structural Differences Between Traditional Print and Digital Environments

Traditional Print	Digital Environments
Table of contents provides support for identifying and locating broad specific topics within a fixed location	• Semantic information and structural labels for hyperlinks within digital environments are often unclear since there are fewer context clues to guide the reader's anticipation about where a hyperlink may lead • Readers may enter anywhere within a website from countless origins
• Content is presented in a fixed linear format as determined by the author • Text structure is usually consistent within the text • Font color, size, shape, and background color may vary but are fixed and static	• Separates content from the way it's displayed, making the text flexible in several key ways • Process of navigating through digital environments is not fixed, it changes within and between sites, and is determined by the reader • Font color, size, shape, and background color vary and may change • May include audio and video • May change daily in structure, form, and content or may disappear entirely • Reader may encounter advertisements, broken links, and access to an infinite amount of information completely unrelated to their intended reading purpose
All written text is bias to a certain degree, but since the text is fixed and static, the author's agenda—explicit or implicit—is fully accessible as inferred by the reader	Hyperlinks can link to multimedia presentations that are connected to the text in complex ways or are politically, socially, or economically motivated on a local, national, or international level

Table 1.1. Structural Differences Between Traditional Print and Digital Environments (continued)

Traditional Print	Digital Environments
Content in its entirety can be previewed prior to reading	• Digital text can be linked for access to other pages within the same website or externally • The actual content of hypertext is hidden beneath multiple layers of information
Intertextual connections are often implicitly embedded by the author and are up to the reader to infer	Intertextual connections are made more explicit, external, physical, and immediate via hyperlinks by the author
Headings and subheadings are used to indicate changes in topic or content and static images, diagrams, maps, etc., are used to enhance or add meaning or understanding to the text	Icons and interactive images, diagrams, or maps may provide a visual representation of a hyperlink, rather than a textual one

closed environments are software programs such as integrated learning systems, CD-ROM storybooks, encyclopedias, or databases. In an open environment, anything that's openly accessible on the Internet becomes available on the screen. There are pros and cons to each environment.

Closed environments do not usually contain advertisements, links that change from one day to the next, or pathways to information that is outside the realm of their intended purpose. Links within closed environments can be used to embed a variety of learning supports such as prompts to stop and predict, summarize, question, or visualize; definitions of key words; and external websites with additional information. Research-based learning strategies can become part of a text, helping students gain meaning (Dalton & Proctor, 2008; Dalton & Rose, 2008).

In contrast, open environments are part of a complex open-ended information system that changes daily in structure, form, and content. A combination of advertisements, propaganda, questionable authorship and quality, and multimedia must be navigated and negotiated by the reader.

At first, the choice between closed and open environments seems simple. Yet even though computer software provides many advantages for students and teachers, it is the Internet and other ICTs that have the greatest potential. Leu, Kinzer, Coiro, and Cammack (2004) state,

> Simply using technology in the classroom does not assure that students are acquiring the new literacies they require. Using . . . software packages designed to support the acquisition of foundational literacies will not prepare students for the new literacies of the Internet and other ICTs. Using these instructional technologies does nothing to develop the essential skills, strategies, and dispositions that define the new literacies. (p. 1600)

The Reader

According to the RAND Study Group (2002), readers bring to the act of reading their

> cognitive capabilities (attention, memory, critical analytic ability, inferencing, visualization); motivation (a purpose for reading, interest in the content, self-efficacy as a reader); knowledge (vocabulary and topic knowledge, linguistic and discourse knowledge, knowledge of comprehension strategies); and experiences. (p. xiv)

Cognitive capabilities, motivation, knowledge, and experiences vary considerably among readers and even within an individual reader as a function of the particular text being read and the reading activity. Fox (2009) reviewed 45 studies of how readers of all ages approach, process, and construct mental representations of informational text, depending on the reader's reading ability, level of schooling, relevant prior knowledge, and interest. Fox made four discoveries that I summarize as:

1. Inexperienced, less able or less knowledgeable readers made unhelpful connections to inaccurate or irrelevant prior knowledge.
2. Knowledge of text structures and expectations related to familiarity with typical texts was an important resource for readers.
3. Quality rather than quantity of strategy use varied depending on level of reading, school experience, and prior knowledge.
4. Quality of goal setting and comprehension monitoring was associated with interest.

The question is whether the attributes employed by the successful readers are the same, different, or more multifaceted in digital environments. Interestingly, distinct parallels exist between Fox's 2009 review and one of the only studies conducted to date of online reading. Coiro and Dobler (2007) examined the reading process of 13 skilled 6th-graders who were asked to locate, critically evaluate for relevancy, and synthesize information from an open Internet environment. Coiro and Dobler found that successful Internet reading experiences appeared to simultaneously require both similar and more complex applications of prior knowledge sources, inferential reasoning strategies, self-regulated reading, and affective variables related to efficacy and motivation.

The first significant finding from the study indicated that skilled readers negotiated within four sources of prior knowledge: subject topics, knowledge of informational text, web-based search engines, and informational website structures. The first two sources of prior knowledge, subject topics (e.g., vocabulary) and knowledge of informational text, are similar to printed text. Topical knowledge assisted the students in constructing a meaningful context within which to locate an answer and in generating search terms, negotiating search results, and inferring from hyperlinked vocabulary words. Knowledge of informational text provided the readers with a familiar organizational context within which to construct meaning. Two additional sources of prior knowledge were web-based search engines and informational website structures, both of which are not employed when reading traditional print texts.

The second significant finding was a high incidence of multilevel forward inferential reasoning due to the lack of traditional previewing strategies or context clues. When selecting hyperlinks, readers were required to anticipate the possible directions the text could take and then, to select what they considered would best fit within the external text they were constructing, before continuing on with their internal meaning construction. Coiro and Dobler (2007) point out that "an increased need to make forward inferences about *text* appeared to compound an already complex process of making bridging inferences about *content* in a manner that may prompt additional complexities to the process of reading online" (p. 242).

The study also found that a third important factor related to forward inferential reading is self-regulated reading. Skilled Internet readers must be able to regulate their movement between

1. Newer online search and evaluation processes that typically occur very rapidly across hundreds of short Internet texts, and
2. less spontaneous, more traditional self-regulation strategies within longer text passages that require more time and effort (p. 242).

Coiro and Dobler (2007) state, "These complexities, then, introduce a new metacognitive regulatory strategy required to combat the motivation of efficiency and spontaneity in order to ultimately slow down and read for meaning" (p. 243). Thus, motivation, the fourth key finding of the study, is very important. Readers' previous experience with the Internet, like conventional print, can affect how successfully they manipulate different aspects of the Web to create meaning. Reinking (2001) asserts:

> Electronic texts that exploit multimedia inherently foster engagement because they naturally promote an active orientation to reading, are easier to read for more readers, fulfill a broad range of social and psychological needs, and more naturally make reading a creative, playful, and less serious activity. (p. 216)

The fact that the majority of children approach the Internet with the attitude that it is "creative, playful, and less serious" may be the reason only a few children use the Internet to explore interests or to find information. As mentioned, the difference may be the way children think about themselves while engaged in the reading activity. However, classroom teachers can help children acquire new literacies that allow them to engage with digital environments as a learning resource.

The Activity

According to the RAND Study Group (2002), the reading activity defines what readers are to do with the text and includes:

- one or more purposes or tasks
- operations to process the text (decoding, higher-level linguistic and semantic processing, and self-monitoring for comprehension)

- outcomes of performing the activity (short term: increase in knowledge, solution to a problem, engagement with the text; long term: increase in knowledge, improved reading comprehension, and engagement with the text)

Of course, engagement with the reading activity is dependent on the text features and the reader's capabilities, as discussed. However, the reading process—or the reader's ability to use information from the language cueing systems (structures and patterns built into the English language) of syntax, semantics, pragmatics, and graphophonics—is also extremely important. Table 1.2 provides a comparison of the use of the cueing systems when the context changes from print to digital. Overall, the addition of varied and animated text, images, hyperlinks, and multimedia adds to the cueing systems from which a reader can draw to make meaning. However, for this information to be meaningful, the reader must make purposeful choices of relevant hyperlinks, icons, and interactive text, and then integrate the information from these multiple knowledge structures into existing knowledge structures. It's easy to see how the digital environment not only supports but challenges readers. Keep in mind that negative experiences in digital environments can develop into poor attitudes toward reading online, just as with reading traditional print. Table 1.2 lists some possible supports and challenges.

Digital environments require readers to take a much more active role in determining the quality and coherence of the texts they read. Thus, knowing when and why to click a particular hyperlink or icon, listen to an audio, or watch a video is a strategic process that influences comprehension. The unique nature of digital texts require readers to use different comprehension strategies than with traditional print texts.

Students do more than just read digital texts, however. As Shirky (2010) notes:

> When you buy a machine that lets you consume digital content, you also buy a machine to produce it. Further, you can share material with your friends, and you can talk about what you consumed or produced or shared. These aren't additional features; they are part of the basic package. (p. 22)

Writing and communicating are part of this basic package.

Writing and Communicating

There was a time not long ago in which the only way to engage with the Internet was to view information. This phase of Internet development has been coined Web 1.0. The advent of web applications that facilitate the interactive and collaborative creation of content ushered in Web 2.0, or the read/write web. Blogs and wikis are two examples of Web 2.0 applications in which the reader is able to create, add, or edit content. Students can create, respond, summarize, annotate or reflect in writing, but the process starts with reading. This reciprocity between reading and writing plays an integral role in comprehension when writing and communicating on the Internet (Boyd & Ellison, 2007; Forte & Bruckman, 2006; Lewis & Fabos, 2005).

Blogging, for example, "richly combines the invitation to speak your mind with the opportunity to mix it up with other minds" (Rosenberg, 2009, p. 336). This reciprocal process requires reading as much as writing, and listening as much as speaking.

Table 1.2. The Cueing Systems Within Traditional Print and Digital Environments

Traditional Print	Digital Environments
Perceptual Cycle	
• Brain uses images from the eye • Images influence what we perceive • If what we perceive doesn't match expectations, we send the eye back to the text for more visual input	• Brain uses images from the eyes and sound from the ears • Images/sound influence what we perceive • If what we perceive doesn't match expectations, we send the eye/ears back to the screen for more textual, visual, and/or auditory input
Semantic Cycle	
• Brain shifts between processing language and processing meaning • Reader uses information from the text and information from background • Reader integrates experiential, interpersonal, and textual meaning	• Brain shifts between processing language and processing meaning • Reader uses information from the text, audio, and/or images and information from background • Reader integrates experiential, interpersonal, and textual/auditory/visual meaning
Visual Cycle	
• Eye fixates at various points along text • Eye picks up enough graphic information to make predictions • Eye sends information to the brain	• Eye fixates at various points along text/image • Eye/ear picks up enough graphic/visual/auditory information to make predictions • Eye/ear sends information to the brain
Syntactic Cycle	
• Reader brings rules of language to assign grammar to the text • Reader uses surface structure to assign deep structure to get to meaning	• Reader brings rules of language/semiotics to assign grammar to the text or meaning to audio and/or images • Reader uses surface structure to assign deep structure to get to meaning

Adapted from Davenport, M. R. (2002). *Miscues not mistakes.* Portsmouth, NH: Heinemann.

Many believe the reciprocal nature of the read/write web has created a new genre of writing. Richardson (2010) has termed this new genre "connective writing." Students who compose online learn to:

- read critically because, as they read, they look for important ideas to write about
- think critically as they consider their audience and clarify the purpose of the writing; evaluate and synthesize information across multiple sources; find and articulate relevance of connections to include or link to
- make editorial decisions such as finding and identifying accurate and trustworthy sources of information and correctness of writing
- anticipate the responses of those who read their writing

The collaboration between reader and writer fundamentally changes the way readers view themselves. When reading almost anything on the web, the reader can "talk back" to the writer—and vice versa. In Thompson's 2009 article, Stanford University Professor of Writing and Rhetoric Andrea Lunsford is quoted as saying, "I think we're in the midst of a literacy revolution the likes of which we haven't seen since Greek civilization" (website, ¶ 3). Through the Stanford Study of Writing, Lunsford and her team of researchers have found that college students today write far more than any previous generation. They also discovered that students today almost always write for (and prefer to write for) an audience—persuading, organizing, and debating—as opposed to a teacher. Therefore, the expanded role of audience in online writing, both addressed (teacher) and invoked (the world), balances the creativity of the writer with the different but equally important, creativity of the reader.

Writing and communicating online changes how readers see themselves. They are no longer passive recipients of information but active creators and distributors of knowledge. Active participants, perhaps motivated by the opportunity to engage in meaningful reading and writing, approach an event as if their presence matters.

The Social Context

The context in which students learn is much more than just the classroom setting. Children come to school with vast differences in their social and cultural backgrounds—economic, ethnic, racial, and linguistic—and varied experiences with literacy influenced by the sociocultural context in which they live at home. More important, children do not leave this cultural perspective at the schoolhouse door. They bring assumptions, values, and attitudes toward reading and literacy, and from homes in which they experienced how language is used and knowledge communicated. Cultural and life experiences are the basis of people's theories and the way they organize experiences (Piaget, 1926; Wood, 1998).

As children engage in new experiences, existing memory structures in the brain, or schema, are reshaped, affecting the child's linguistic, cognitive, social, and emotional development. According to Ryan and Cooper (2013), "Knowledge cannot be given directly from the teacher to the learner, but must be constructed by the learner and reconstructed as new information becomes available" (p. 307). Learning is not a result of development but development itself. From this perspective, a child's potential for learning is revealed and even realized through interactions with those who possess greater knowledge.

Sometimes, however, those who possess greater knowledge about technology are not always teachers. The technological knowledge that many students bring to the classroom can intimidate some teachers. As a result, these teachers may leave technology instruction to the computer teacher; however, the computer teacher seldom has the expertise or time to teach the new literacies described so far in this chapter. Once-weekly classes are not enough to scaffold the learning taking place in the classroom. It is the classroom teacher who is ideally positioned to teach new literacies.

To prepare children to successfully interact with digital environments, literacy teachers can do much to scaffold students' acquisition of the new literacies required to comprehend, compose, and communicate online. The social context influences the text, the reader, and the reading activity. Many online environments allow students to collaborate and construct knowledge together; and provide a space for students locally, nationally, and internationally to work together virtually. As Richardson (2010) writes:

> [W]hen we share online, we create the potential for connections in ways that were simply not possible a few years ago. And in the context of those connections, we can form groups around our various passions and interests, a capability that fundamentally changes almost everything. (p. 3)

It may be messy at first, as teachers grapple with challenges that arise and find that there may be more questions than answers. Yet there is solace in knowing that we are providing students with the experiences they will need to be literate in 2020 and beyond.

The next chapter provides a framework to assist teachers in using their content and pedagogical expertise in flexible ways to create a literacy curriculum that includes the instruction of new literacies within digital environments.

CHAPTER 2

A Framework for Literacy 2.0 Thinking

> I have always been wary of all of the education technology out there. For one thing, I think that the overwhelming volume of it causes a "paralysis of choice" where those that are trying to become techno-literate teachers throw up their hands in disgust and just say "too much!"
>
> —Tim Holt, *Six Items in Your Digital Suitcase: Opinion* (2010)

Tim's "paralysis of choice" is often a common reaction among educators. There are just too many tools and resources to choose from, so rather than randomly, inadequately, or superficially use them, teachers often use none at all. Teaching is a complex process. Koehler and Mishra (2008) contend that teaching "is a classic example of an ill-structured discipline with a high level of variability across situations as well as a dense, context-dependent inter-connectedness between knowledge and practice" (p. 4). Teachers, who sit at the center of this "ill-structured discipline," often use frameworks for thinking about these complexities. Two frameworks will be discussed in this chapter, Technological Pedagogical Content Knowledge (TPACK), developed by Koehler and Mishra (2008) for thinking about the integration of technology into the curriculum and NCTE's 21st Century Literacies Framework for thinking about planning, supporting, and assessing student learning. Finally, the Internet reciprocal teaching (IRT) routine will be discussed as a way to create effective lessons that support teaching the skills, strategies, and dispositions necessary for learning to effectively read, write, and communicate in digital environments.

THE TECHNOLOGICAL PEDAGOGICAL CONTENT KNOWLEDGE FRAMEWORK

Rather than beginning with technology, the TPACK framework asks teachers to begin with content or the curriculum goals. Once teachers have in mind *what* they are teaching, they move to selecting the pedagogy or instructional strategies and assessments that will be most effective for teaching and learning the curriculum goals. After thinking through curriculum goals, teachers should consider whether technology can support these goals and instructional strategies (see Figure 2.1). Teachers must have knowledge of technology and its pros and cons; however, when their starting point is the literacy curriculum and appropriate instructional strategies for teaching the curriculum, then the selection of technology becomes purposeful.

Figure 2.1. The Technological Pedagogical Content Knowledge Framework

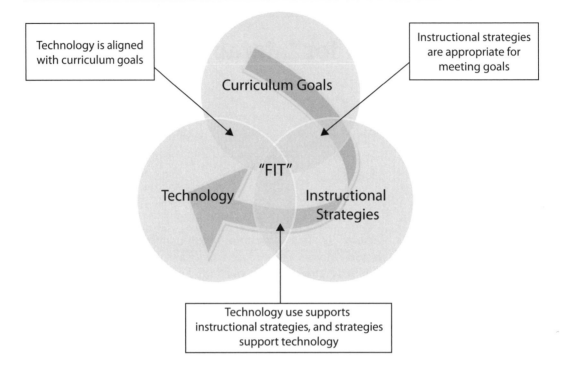

Teachers have an in-depth understanding of the content and pedagogy of literacy instruction. However, it is within the context of digital environments that new understandings of content and pedagogy come into play. The next three sections, content, pedagoagy and technology, will address the TPACK components as they relate to literacy instruction. The final section will discuss the integration of these three components in a "just right" fit that deepens and extends student learning.

Content: Curriculum Goals

For all but five states in the United States, the Common Core State Standards (CCSS) serve as the literacy curriculum standards. The K–5 English Language Arts (ELA) Standards define what students should understand and be able to do in reading, writing, listening and speaking, language and media, and technology by the end of each grade. However, reading is not an academic discipline like math or science for which standards usually constitute specialized knowledge of concepts, taxonomies, and theories. Rather, the ELA standards constitute procedural knowledge encompassing certain processes, strategies, and routines. Therefore, a science teacher might use *inferring* to understand the results of an experiment, whereas a literacy teacher will teach students the strategy of inferring.

The ELA standards are organized around a set of College and Career Readiness (CCR) anchor standards. The introduction to the ELA CCR standards provides a portrait of students who meet the standards. The description of media and technology follows:

> Students employ technology thoughtfully to enhance their reading, writing, speaking, listening, and language use. They tailor their searches online to acquire useful information efficiently, and they integrate what they learn using technology with what they learn offline. They are familiar with the strengths and limitations of various technological tools and mediums and can select and use those best suited to their communication goals. (ELA Introduction, ¶ 7)

With these CCR anchor standards in mind, a key design consideration for the grade specific standards was to blend the research and media skills into the standards as a whole:

> The need to conduct research and to produce and consume media is embedded into every aspect of today's curriculum. In like fashion, research and media skills and understandings are embedded throughout the Standards rather than treated in a separate section. (ELA Introduction to Key Design Considerations, ¶ 6)

Figure 2.2 lists the ELA standards across K–5 that include media or technology. However, technology tools and resources can and should be integrated into the instruction of other ELA standards, even those that do not specifically state the use of media or technology.

Figure 2.2. K–5 ELA Standards That Include Technology

READING LITERATURE

Integration of Knowledge and Ideas

5.7: Analyze how visual and multimedia elements contribute to the meaning, tone, or beauty of a text (e.g., graphic novel, multimedia presentation of fiction, folktale, myth, poem).

READING INFORMATION TEXT

Integration of Knowledge and Ideas

3.5: Use text features and search tools (e.g., key words, sidebars, hyperlinks) to locate information relevant to a given topic efficiently.

4.7: Interpret information presented visually, orally, or quantitatively (e.g., in charts, graphs, diagrams, time lines, animations, or interactive elements on webpages) and explain how the information contributes to an understanding of the text in which it appears.

5.7: Draw on information from multiple print or digital sources, demonstrating the ability to locate an answer to a question quickly or to solve a problem efficiently.

Figure 2.2. K–5 ELA Standards That Include Technology (continued)

WRITING STANDARDS

Text Types and Purposes

4.2: Write informative/explanatory texts to examine a topic and convey ideas and information clearly. Introduce a topic clearly and group related information in paragraphs and sections; include formatting (e.g., headings), illustrations, and multimedia when useful to aiding comprehension.

5.2: Introduce a topic clearly, provide a general observation and focus, and group related information logically; include formatting (e.g., headings), illustrations, and multimedia when useful to aiding comprehension.

Production and Distribution of Writing

3.6: With guidance and support from adults, use technology to produce and publish writing (using keyboarding skills) as well as to interact and collaborate with others.

4.6 and 5.6: With some guidance and support from adults, use technology, including the Internet, to produce and publish writing as well as to interact and collaborate with others; demonstrate sufficient command of keyboarding skills to type a minimum of one page in a single sitting.

SPEAKING AND LISTENING STANDARDS

Comprehension and Collaboration

K.2: Confirm understanding of a text read aloud or information presented orally or through other media by asking and answering questions about key details and requesting clarification if something is not understood.

1.2: Ask and answer questions about key details in a text read aloud or information presented orally or through other media.

2.2: Recount or describe key ideas or details from a text read aloud or information presented orally or through other media.

3.2: Determine the main ideas and supporting details of a text read aloud or information presented in diverse media and formats, including visually, quantitatively, and orally.

4.2: Paraphrase portions of a text read aloud or information presented in diverse media and formats, including visually, quantitatively, and orally.

5.2: Summarize a written text read aloud or information presented in diverse media and formats, including visually, quantitatively, and orally.

Presentation of Knowledge and Ideas

5.5: Include multimedia components (e.g., graphics, sound) and visual displays in presentations when appropriate to enhance the development of main ideas or themes.

Source: National Governors Association Center for Best Practices, Council of Chief State School Officers (2010). *Common Core State Standards* (*English/Language Arts*). National Governors Association Center for Best Practices, Council of Chief State School Officers, Washington, DC.

Pedagogy: Instructional Strategies and Assessments

As mentioned previously, the ELA standards represent a set of processes, strategies, and routines for becoming an effective reader, writer, and communicator. Therefore, when teaching a strategy such as inferring, teachers are selecting the best instructional strategies for teaching a strategy. This requires mental "unpacking" of these processes.

Adults who are proficient readers possess a highly abstract level of *compressed* knowledge that is automatically and implicitly recalled. In fact, trying to remain cognizant of the processes enacted when reading—decoding, analyzing text structure, using specific comprehension strategies—would impede the fluency and comprehension necessary to process text efficiently. As Phelps and Schilling (2004) point out,

> If asked, few adult readers could "unpack" what they are doing. Even fewer could identify the knowledge of text, language, and reading processes from which they draw as they read. Even competent adult readers require additional knowledge about text, language, and reading processes in order to teach reading. (p. 35)

Thus, to teach a strategy for reading, writing, and communicating in both traditional and digital environments, teachers must be aware of the process that few adult readers possess and then make the invisible process visible to students. As discussed in Chapter 1, strategies for reading, writing, and communicating in traditional and digital environments are similar and different. Think-alouds, modeling, demonstrations, and explanations are effective instructional strategies often employed by teachers to make thinking visible for digital and print texts. Then, over time, they gradually release responsibility to the students by scaffolding, or supporting, their attempts until students understand and can flexibly use the strategy independently. Additionally, the teachers' ability to select appropriate instructional strategies includes knowledge of students' prior knowledge and the establishment of conditions that promote learning (e.g., creating a literate environment, valuing diversity, and implementing classroom management strategies).

Of course, without assessment, meaningful instruction that meets all students' needs is impossible. Assessment informs all instructional decisions. Teachers must use their knowledge of literacy processes to appropriately assess children. For example, when assessing comprehension, teachers must understand the process of constructing meaning from text—including strategies for reading, monitoring, and responding—and then carefully apply that knowledge to design assessments. Literacy learning is a complex and multifaceted process, so accurately capturing a student's literacy knowledge and behaviors requires multiple assessments that are systematic, ongoing, and fully integrated into the instructional environment. Authentic assessments may include observational notes, checklists, conferences, rubrics, and portfolios. Assessments specific to capturing knowledge of digital literacies have largely not been created; however, many of the aforementioned assessments can be adapted for this purpose (assessment will be discussed in Chapter 9).

It is the literacy teacher's "unpacked" understanding of the processes of reading and the ability to use this knowledge in varied contexts, interactions, and practices that ultimately make him or her uniquely qualified to prepare students to read, write, and communicate effectively in digital environments.

Technology

Most U.S. schools have access to computers that are connected to the Internet and a select number of other technologies. Gray, Thomas, and Lewis (2010) report that, in 2009, 97% of K–12 teachers had one or more computers located in the classroom every day, 93% had Internet access to those computers, 84% had an LCD or DLP projector, 78% had a digital camera, and 51% had an interactive whiteboard. Yet, simply providing teachers with access to technology does not give them the preparation they may need to integrate the Internet and electronic equipment into their instruction.

Just as teachers use their expertise to carefully and intentionally select the best and most effective instructional strategies to meet students' literacy needs, so should they select technology tools and resources. As we will discuss in Chapter 10, there are many ways to stay abreast of effective technology tools, resources, and applications for literacy instruction. Table 2.1 provides an overview of most of the hardware, software, and online applications that will be discussed throughout this book.

It is important for teachers to be aware of the level of Internet access available in their schools. Firewalls and blocking software may limit access to the Internet sites

Table 2.1. Definitions of Selected Hardware, Software, and Online Applications

Hardware, Software, or Online Application	Definition
Chat room	An online venue where people who share a common interest can communicate in real time by typing out conversations on their keyboards
Cloud Computing	Internet-based computing where different services such as storage and applications are delivered to computers and devices through the Internet
Discussion board	Online bulletin boards where people can post and respond to messages
Information communication technology (ICT)	An umbrella term that includes any communication device or application such as cellular phone, personal digital assistant (PDA), MP3 player, and computer and network hardware and software
Interactive whiteboard	A large interactive screen connected to a computer and projector; screen is touch sensitive, which means users can control it using a finger or pen as a mouse
Instant messenger	Allows two people to have a short conversation instantly
Mobile applications or apps	Allow connections and posting to email, blogs, and social networking sites from mobile devices such as cell phones

Table 2.1. Definitions of Selected Hardware, Software, and Online Applications (continued)

Hardware, Software, or Online Application	Definition
MP3	An audio file in which the amount of data is reduced or compressed for transmission
Podcast	An audio file, usually in MP3 format, that is available online, and can be downloaded and listened to at the user's convenience
RSS/aggregator	RSS, or Really Simple Syndication, collects news from various websites, and provides it to a computer in a simple form; examples include Bloglines, SharpReader, and NetNewsWire
Social bookmarking	A central online site which allows users to add, annotate, edit, and share bookmarks of web documents. Examples of social bookmarking sites include: Diigo, Delicious, Webnotes, and Evernote
Social networking	Facebook, MySpace, Ning, LinkedIn, Twitter, Plurk, Goodreads, and Edmondo are examples of sites where people can share their lives via writing, photos, videos, and audio
Video conferencing	The use of technologies such as Skype or Google+ that allow people in two or more remote locations to communicate by simultaneous via two-way video and audio signals
Webcam	Video camera whose content is fed to a website
Weblog, or blog	An interactive online journal whose writer is known as a "blogger" and the process of keeping an online diary is known as "blogging"
Web-based software	Software streamed from the Internet rather than downloaded to a computer (e.g., Google Docs word processor, spreadsheet, presentation, form, and data storage service that allows the integration of video, audio, text, and graphics such as Glogster and Voicethread)
Wiki	Server program that allows anyone to edit or add content

and software programs discussed throughout this book. Teachers should talk to the instructional resource person in their school or district, show him or her what they are doing and why, and find out if there are ways to get access for particular purposes.

As discussed in Chapter 1, the decision to use technology comes not only from knowing what technological tools and resources are available, but understanding the affordances and constraints of technology for literacy learning. Technology can deepen many important aspects of literacy for children in ways not afforded by traditional print. Mohr and Orr (2009) discuss the power of audience for 5th-grade students who wrote about their reading more frequently on blogs than in their readers' notebooks:

When students simply wrote in their readers' notebooks, their sole discussion partner was their teacher, and opportunities for broad discussions about texts were limited. Blogs allowed the conversation to expand and this broader range allowed for dialogue that cultivated a variety of perspectives and a deeper level of thinking. (Increasing Reading and Deepening Understanding section)

Unfortunately, technology is rarely used in ways that promote deep thinking and reflection. Gray, Thomas, and Lewis (2010) reported that a majority of K–12 teachers use software for administering tests (44%), simulation programs (33%), drill/practice programs (50%), and subject-specific programs (56%). Only a small percentage use blogs and/or wikis (16%), social networking sites (8%), or online bulletin boards for class discussion (11%). Yet, many of these read/write web resources can be used to build relationships with other students, to pose and solve problems collaboratively, and to design and share information for global communities.

However, other aspects of literacy are constrained by technology. Wolf and Brazillai (2009) stress the danger of the emphasis on immediacy, information overloading, and media-driven digital culture to deep reading. They define deep reading as "the array of sophisticated processes that propel comprehension and that include inferential and deductive reasoning, analogical skills, critical analysis, reflection, and insight" (p. 33). As discussed in the previous section, the proficient adult reader is able to initiate these processes almost instantly, but the young reader needs years to develop them. Wolf and Brazillai warn:

> An early immersion in reading that is largely online tends to reward certain cognitive skills, such as multitasking, and habituate the learner to immediate information gathering and quick attention shifts, rather than to deep reflection and ordinal thought. (p. 36)

Literacy teachers can assist students with learning to read deeply online by selecting instructional strategies and digital tools that teach them how to manage, analyze, and synthesize multiple streams of simultaneous information and to create, critique, analyze and evaluate multimedia texts. Yet, as Wolf and Brazillai (2009) note, "nothing replaces the unique contributions of print literacy for the development of the full panoply of the slower, constructive, cognitive process that invite children to create their own whole works . . ." (p. 37). The bottom line is that technology should not drive instruction. Instead, the desired curricular outcomes and students' needs should be the driving factors. Understanding how technology and reading content influence and constrain one another is essential to effective instruction and appropriate selection of technology that promotes deep reading.

TPACK: The "Just Right" Fit

True technology integration comes from understanding and negotiating the relationships among curriculum, instructional strategies, and technology to achieve a "just right" fit that deepens and extends student learning (Koehler & Mishra, 2008).

21ST-CENTURY LITERACIES FRAMEWORK

TPACK provides a framework for thinking about the intentional integration of technology that is a "just right" fit in the literacy curriculum. However, 21st-century literacies do not equal technology alone. There are many skills (creativity, communication, collaboration, critical thinking, and comprehension), strategies (identifying important questions, locating relevant information, crucially evaluating, synthesizing, and communicating) and dispositions (persistence, flexibility, collaboration, critical stance, and reflection) required to effectively participate, collaborate, and communicate today and in the future.

The National Council of Teachers of English (NCTE) has taken a leadership role in recognizing the need for 21st-century skills by developing a framework for 21st-century literacies (www.ncte.org/governance/21stcenturyframework). NCTE's 21st Century Literacies Framework (2008) pulls together the skills, strategies, and dispositions important to planning, supporting, and assessing students' acquisition of new literacies. The framework is unique in that rather than provide a list of requirements, it uses questioning as a tool to guide thinking, design and reflection on practice. Below are the six elements of the framework and a sample of the questions for each.

Develop proficiency with the tools of technology

- Do students use technology as a tool for communication, research, and creation of new works?
- Do students take risks and try new things with tools available to them?
- Do students, independently and collaboratively, solve problems as they arise in their work?

Build relationships with others to pose and solve problems collaboratively and cross-culturally

- Do students work in a group in ways that allow them to create new knowledge or to solve problems that can't be created or solved individually?
- Do students work in groups whose members have diverse perspectives and areas of expertise?
- Do students build on one another's thinking to gain new understanding?

Design and share information for global communities that have a variety of purposes

- Do students use inquiry to ask questions and solve problems?
- Do students critically analyze a variety of information from a variety of sources?
- Do students publish in ways that meet the needs of a particular, authentic audience?

Manage, analyze, and synthesize multiple streams of simultaneously presented information

- Do students create new ideas using knowledge gained?
- Do students analyze the credibility of information and its appropriateness in meeting their needs?
- Do students synthesize information from a variety of sources?

Create, critique, analyze, and evaluate multimedia texts

- Do students use tools to create new thinking or to communicate original perspectives?
- Do students evaluate multimedia sources for the effects of visuals, sounds, hyperlinks, and other features on the text's meaning or emotional impact?
- Do students evaluate their own multimedia works?

Attend to the ethical responsibilities required by complex environments

- Do students share information in ways that consider all sources?
- Do students practice the safe and legal use of technology?
- Do students create products that are both informative and ethical?

Implications of the Framework

The framework's questions prompt teachers to reflect on their literacy curriculum, instruction, and assessment practices; allowing them to integrate strategies and activities that provide students the opportunity to develop 21st-century literacies. In this way, the framework supports and deepens literacy practices, allowing teachers to become thoughtful instructional designers. Washburn (2010) writes, "*Instructional design* differs from lesson *planning*, the term we traditionally use to describe a teacher's pre-instruction preparation. Designers communicate by *intentionally* combining elements" (pp. 2–3).

The next section provides an overview of an instructional routine that employs the gradual release of responsibility model. The routine will assist teachers with designing instruction that provides students with opportunities for learning the skills, strategies and dispositions of new literacies.

INTERNET RECIPROCAL TEACHING

Reciprocal teaching (Palincsar & Brown, 1984) is an instructional routine that has been found to be highly effective for modeling and providing support for students to use comprehension strategies (Hattie, 2009). Reciprocal teaching takes the form of a dialogue between teachers and students around sections of text. The dialogue is structured by the use of four strategies: summarizing, questioning, clarifying, and predicting. At the start of reciprocal teaching, the teacher provides extensive modeling of the strategies. As the teacher releases responsibility for using the strategies to the students, the teacher and students take turns assuming the role of teacher in leading this dialogue. According to Duke and Pearson (2002), a typical reciprocal teaching session includes the following:

1. The student's review of the main points from the previous session's reading or, if the reading is new, make predictions about the text based on the title and other information.
2. All students independently read the first paragraph of the text silently.
3. A student, assigned to act as teacher:
   a. asks a question about the paragraph,
   b. summarizes the paragraph,
   c. asks for clarification, if needed, and
   d. predicts what might be in the next paragraph. (p. 225)

The teacher serves as a guide throughout the process and reminds students why these strategies are important and how they will help them in their reading. As time goes on, students assume increasing control over strategy use, eventually using the strategies with little or no teacher support.

According to Oczkus (2010), "Reciprocal teaching is a flexible tool that you use to strengthen and differentiate the comprehension instruction in any core reading program or curriculum model" (p. 243). McVerry, Zawlinski, and O'Byrne (2009) have adapted reciprocal teaching to support the skills, strategies, and dispositions necessary for learning to effectively read, write, and communicate in digital environments. Their adaptation, known as Internet reciprocal teaching (IRT), builds on the same principles as reciprocal teaching; that is, the gradual release of responsibility to students, group discussion, and sharing strategies are central to both approaches. However, with IRT, instruction revolves around building the online reading comprehension strategies of questioning, locating, evaluating, synthesizing, and communicating.

McVerry, Zawlinski, and O'Byrne (2009) present a three-phase model for implementing IRT (see Table 2.2). Phase 1 focuses on technology tools, and will vary in the time it takes to complete based on the students' experiences and needs. In this phase, the responsibility of modeling strategies lies with the teacher.

Phase 2 is a collaborative phase during which teachers and students conduct think-aloud demonstrations and minilessons. Teacher modeling in the first half of the phase gives way to student modeling in the latter half. Students take responsibility for teaching their peers a variety of online reading comprehension strategies. Instruction also begins to move from search skills to critical evaluation and synthesis skills.

Phase 3 involves students working both individually and in small groups, using strategies and skills from the previous phases to develop lines of inquiry around curricular topics. This type of project requires clear questions, multiple reliable sources, citations, and a final product that communicates that information to others.

Table 2.2. Three-Phase Model for Implementing Internet Reciprocal Teaching

Gradual Release of Responsibility	Phase 1 Develop proficiency with the tools of technology	Phase 2 Develop proficiency with strategies of new literacies	Phase 3 Develop proficiency with using skills and strategies for independent learning
Teacher Modeling	<ul><li>Computer basics</li><li>Word processing skills</li><li>Web searching</li><li>Navigation basics</li><li>Email</li></ul>		
Teacher and Student Demonstrations		<ul><li>Identify questions</li><li>Locate relevant information</li><li>Critically evaluate</li><li>Synthesize</li><li>Communicate</li></ul>	
Independent Practice			Using strategies individually and in small groups to:<ul><li>Create</li><li>Communicate</li><li>Collaborate</li><li>Think critically</li><li>Comprehend</li></ul>
	Ongoing development of collaborative skills and ethical dispositions		
	Ongoing assessment of skills, strategies, and dispositions		

The reading contexts in which instruction and guided and independent practice take place on the Internet varies depending on the literacy curriculum and students' needs. However, IRT lessons typically progress from easy to more complex across contexts. For example, a teacher might start by helping students navigate within a webpage and then progress to navigating between two webpages and then multiple webpages. An additional goal across all lessons should be to help students understand that the Internet can be an important learning resource.

USING THE FRAMEWORKS AND IRT ROUTINE TO DESIGN CURRICULUM

The following is an example of how one 2nd-grade teacher used the TPACK and NCTE 21st Century Literacies Frameworks and the IRT routine to design instruction to meet the needs of her students.

Debbie was planning her poetry unit that she introduces to her students each April during National Poetry Month. She was looking specifically at CCSS Reading Literature (RL) 2.4: Describe how words and phrases (e.g., regular beats, alliteration, rhymes, repeated lines) supply rhythm and meaning in a story, poem, or song. Critical to students' success in accomplishing this standard is listening to poetry read aloud with appropriate tone, inflection, phrasing, and rhythm. Debbie loves poetry and models effective poetry reading and discusses the elements of each poem that contributes to the rhyme and meaning. She also gives her students the opportunity to talk to one another about these elements after hearing a poem read aloud. During independent reading time, students read and collect favorite poems in their poetry notebooks and then share the poems with one another at the end of the day. Debbie has always found these instructional strategies (reading aloud, modeling, discussion, and independent reading) to be largely effective, but some students are not able to read a poem using appropriate tone, inflection, phrasing, and rhythm, even after weeks of modeling and scaffolded practice.

Following the TPACK framework, Debbie identified the curriculum goal and the instructional strategies she believes are most effective for meeting the goal. The just right technology fit would be a tool that would allow students to record and hear themselves read so they would be able to monitor and adjust their reading to emphasize a poem's rhythm. She researched digital voice recording tools and selected SoundCloud (soundcloud.com), a free, easy-to-use application that allows users to make recordings and to leave recorded comments about their recordings.

Using questions from the NCTE 21st Century Literacy Framework, Debbie thought about the technology knowledge her students would need to use this tool independently. She also thought about how students could work together to gain new understandings by reflecting on their readings and sharing their work with each other. Recording and commenting on their readings allowed the students to evaluate their ability to monitor and adjust their reading when necessary. Additionally, students engaged in self-evaluation and reflection on the process and product that was integrated into the learning process and contributed to students' continued growth.

Debbie followed the steps in the IRT routine to plan her minilesson that included how to use the application and provided a gradual release of responsibility over time. She made sure students understood why they were being asked to record their poetry reading, and provided examples of her recording her own poetry reading, replaying and reflecting on the recording based on what students had previously learned about rhythm. Then several pairs of students recorded their readings each day until everyone in the class had a turn. After all students listened to their recordings (with headphones), they had the opportunity to rerecord if not satisfied or to leave a comment for Debbie as to why the recording met their expectations. Finally, Debbie listened to each recording and left a comment providing formative feedback for each student, which he or she had the opportunity to hear the next day. She uploaded each recording to her online assessment notebook and shared the recordings with parents during parent teacher conferences.

With Debbie's preparation and planning, SoundCloud was a perfect fit. It allowed students to listen and reflect on their own poetry readings and monitor and adjust their readings, which improved their understanding of rhythm and the contributions of rhythm to meaning construction. The recordings also provided Debbie with an opportunity for individual feedback and assessment.

Using the TPACK and NCTE frameworks and IRT routine, teachers become instructional designers. Informed instructional design produces effective teaching, and effective teaching in digital environments is especially important because teachers

> are teaching for some time in the future when the knowledge and skills that are learned in our classes are tested in contexts that we cannot know and with assessments that we cannot design. We need to provide an education that lasts a lifetime. (Halpern & Hakel, 2002, p. 4)

CHAPTER 3

Creating Classroom Community and Connecting with Families

Imagine a student arriving at a new school. Perhaps she has come from a rural setting to an urban one. At first, she will be concerned with getting to know her new environment, the people in it, and the way the culture functions. She will have many questions and often be confused by her new experiences. Interested in learning all about her new school and based on what she knows about school from her past experiences, she will "step into" this new setting and begin to build an understanding—or envisionment—of it. At first she will pull together any "clues" about the school she can find— who the students are and how they are like or different from herself; who her teachers are and their expectations; where her classes are located and how each is organized. She will begin to build her envisionment of this new environment, rethinking or adding to her understanding of the school as she encounters something new.

—Judith Langer and Elizabeth Close,
Improving Literacy Understanding Through Classroom Conversation (2001, p. 7)

In *Improving Literacy Understanding Through Classroom Conversation*, Langer and Close (2001) look at students' envisionments—"the wealth of ideas that people have in their minds at any point in time"—as they relate to literary understanding (p. 6). Langer and Close worked with teachers of grades 1–12 and 1st-year college teachers to learn more about how readers think when they read and discuss literature and how teachers can help students use discussion to think deeply. They found that the processes involved in literary understanding are *as important* as the instructional environments, activities, and interactions that support it. Langer and Close (2001) write:

> In envisionment-building classrooms where students have mutual support systems from teachers and other students, they are given the room to form their own understandings and to use interaction with others to explore horizons of possibilities. (p. 11)

All students who enter the classroom come as members of families, neighborhoods, religious groups, sports teams, clubs, and organizations, each of which is a community of practice, or a place "where human beings *develop competence through their interactions* with each other" (Crafton, 2006, p. 1). Through these interactions, students define their identities. Classrooms are also communities of practice where each student possesses unique knowledge and perspective that pushes the thinking of other students. Specifically, classroom communities of practice:

- allow students to develop positive identities about themselves as learners
- foster the learning of new interactions while also honoring existing ones
- create opportunities for students to contribute their past experiences to the collective knowledge of the group (p. 7)

When teachers develop classroom communities of practice in which students respect the knowledge and contributions of others, they help students understand that learning isn't just about "doing more school" but about participating in practice that matters to them. The following sections discuss the importance of the teacher's language and digital environments in creating classroom communities of practice.

THE IMPORTANCE OF LANGUAGE TO BUILDING CLASSROOM COMMUNITY

As Johnston notes in his classic 2004 book *Choice Words: How Our Language Affects Children's Learning*:

> [E]ach conversational exchange between teacher and student(s) provides building material for children's understanding of a wide range of literate concepts, practices, and possibilities, and helps shape their identities. . . . (p. 10)

The conversation between Coach O and Ben in Chapter 1 is an example of building possibilities through language. After Ben finished reading, Coach O told him, "Good. I think I know what's going on. I can help you" (Armstrong, p. 132). Her response could have been quite different—one that would have expressed Ben's at-risk status as a reader. However, Coach O's response conveys who she is, what her purpose is, and how she will relate to Ben when they read together. Johnston asserts that the words and phrases that turn up in conversations between teachers and students exert considerable power over classroom conversations, and thus over students' literate and intellectual development. Table 3.1 provides categories and examples of productive teacher talk. The examples can have a profound effect on individual learning and classroom communities if used in a reflective, thoughtful, and caring way.

Clearly, the questions and language suggested by Johnston aren't prompts that can be neatly pulled out and used according to a set of protocols. However, they can serve as a springboard for teachers to inquire into classroom practices. When teachers examine their actions, they reflect on their beliefs. If teachers believe, as the premise of this book suggests, that children must acquire the skills, strategies, and dispositions necessary to successfully use and adapt to the rapidly changing ICTs, then conversations and ways of engaging with children must reflect this belief.

Table 3.1. Categories and Examples of Productive Teacher Talk (Johnston, 2004)

Category of Teacher Talk	Example of Teacher Talk
Naming and noticing	
When people are being apprenticed into an activity of any sort, they have to figure out the key features of the activity and their significance . . . . As teachers we socialize children's attention to the significant features of literacy and of learning in different domains. (p. 11)	"Did anyone notice . . . ?" or "What are you noticing?" "I see you know how to . . . " "What kind of text is this?" "You know what I hear you doing just now . . . ? You may not have realized it." "I want you to tell me how it [group discussion] went? What went well? What kinds of questions were raised?"
Identity	
Building an identity means coming to see in ourselves the characteristics of particular categories (and roles) of people and developing a sense of what it feels like to be that sort of person and belong in certain social spaces. (p. 23)	"What a talented young poet you are." "I wonder if, as a writer, you're ready for this." "I bet you're proud of yourself." "What are you doing as a writer today?" "What have you learned most recently as a reader?"
Agency and becoming strategic	
Teacher's conversations with children help the children build the bridges between action and consequence that develop their sense of agency. They show children how, by acting strategically, they accomplish things, and at the same time, that they are the kind of person who accomplishes things. (p. 30)	"How did you figure that out?" "How are you planning to go about this?" "Where are you going with this piece of writing?" "Which part are you sure about and which part are you not sure about?" "You made a conscious choice."
Flexibility and transfer	
Teachers build bridges between activity settings, making it so that the agency a child exercises in one area transfers to another. (p. 44)	"One of the things people do when they start a story is think of what they know. Mathematicians do this . . . Let's try it." "How else . . . ?" "That's like . . . " "What if . . . ?"

Table 3.1. Categories and Examples of Productive Teacher Talk (Johnston, 2004) [continued]

Category of Teacher Talk	Example of Teacher Talk
Knowing	
Teachers use conversational pivots or examples of talk that lead to conversations in which children play a more active role in the ownership and construction of knowledge. (p. 54)	"Let's see if I've got this right" (then summarizes students' extended comments). "That's a very interesting way of looking at it. I hadn't thought about it that way. I'll have to think about it some more." "How did you know?" "How could we check?" "Would you agree with that?"
An evolutionary, democratic learning community	
The social relationships within which children learn are a part of their learning. Children, just like adults, learn better in a supportive environment in which they can risk trying out new strategies and concepts and stretching themselves intellectually. (p. 65)	"How do you think she feels about that?" "You guys say such important things that it amazes me you would talk while others are talking." "I wonder . . . " "Are there any other ways to think about that? Any other opinions?" "What are you thinking? Stop and talk to your neighbor about it."

THE ROLE OF DIGITAL ENVIRONMENTS IN BUILDING CLASSROOM COMMUNITY

As discussed in Chapter 1, the social context for learning to comprehend, compose, and communicate online is critical. Digital environments can be communities of practice in which the "culture of the various groups of users matters enormously for what they expect of one another and how they work together" (Shirky, 2010, p. 28). It can be used for the development of collaborative learning, making it easier for students to see varied perspectives on issues, fostering new meaning construction, and promoting deep self-reflection and dialogue with others (Pena-Shaff, Martin, & Gay, 2001). Yet, using packaged software programs will not create an environment that supports this type of learning. For this transformative learning to occur, "the environment must provide support and the ability to dialogue and critically reflect on the material presented, as well as on the self" (Palloff & Pratt, 2007, p. 185). As discussed, technologies differ in their richness, or the ability to promote interaction among students, teachers, and content that results in enhanced learning. When implemented at developmentally appropriate levels, technology can illustrate the complexity and richness of a real world context, which fosters literacy learning for all students.

ACTIVITIES THAT BUILD CLASSROOM COMMUNITY

A variety of activities that begin the first day of school (or before) and continue throughout the year can provide a range of opportunities and experiences for students to get to know one other, understand each other's perspectives, and learn to work together in many ways.

Digital Storytelling

Digital storytelling and biographies provide authentic opportunities for students to bring their culture into the classroom and share with their classmates and other students around the world. For example, "student of the week" is a common approach many teachers use for students to learn more about one another to build classroom community. Students bring in pictures of themselves, family members, friends, pets, and significant events in their lives, and these pictures are often displayed on a bulletin board. Over the course of many weeks, students get to share their life stories and classmates get to learn more about one another and make connections. Yet much of the richness of students' lives is lost via this single medium. How much more powerful would students' connections be if they were allowed to share video/audio clips and add text, music, or voice recordings? The combination of media allows for a potentially more meaningful connection than would a single image. However, to achieve deeper meaning, students must learn how to connect different sources of information from text, images, video, and audio into existing knowledge structures.

Even primary-age children can learn to create, publish, and share multimedia with each other about important aspects of their lives. Sylvester and Greenidge (2009) found digital storytelling to be a promising tool for supporting struggling writers. By modeling and thinking aloud, teachers can assist children in learning how to use multimedia to make connections, ask questions, communicate ideas, and learn about and from each other. The IRT lessons for this chapter will describe how students can create a multimedia photo or story and learn how to respond to one another's photos or stories in meaningful ways to build community.

IRT LESSON FOR YOUNGER STUDENTS: DIGITAL STORYTELLING

Phase 1: Teacher modeling

Step 1: Planning the lesson. You will need to:

- choose which digital storytelling program to use (e.g., Photo Story, iPhoto, Animoto, VoiceThread)
- decide which photograph you want students to bring

- determine how to collect photographs
- create your own storytelling example
- decide which strategies your students need to navigate through the program

The first step is to decide which technology resource to use. VoiceThread is a free online program and iPad app that allows students to add a caption and audio narration to photos and videos (in addition to many other document types). Additionally, it allows students to comment on one another's photo or videos. The IRT lessons for this chapter employ VoiceThread because it affords more opportunities for students to both create and reflect on their lives and those of their classmates. Privacy settings allow students to share their work with family members or make it available to the public. In addition, emergent and early readers may have trouble reading directions that are included in a particular application that explain how to navigate; however, VoiceThread is predominately visual, is very simple and intuitive, and provides an opportunity for teachers to model the strategic process of navigating through a program.

Next, decide whether to allow students to choose any photo for their VoiceThread or to require a specific picture (e.g., a picture with the students' family, a favorite activity, etc.). Young children who have limited experience using computers and are in emergent or early stages of the reading process should start with one picture with a text caption, audio narration, or both. In this IRT lesson, both are included.

Another planning consideration is how to manage the collection of students' photos. The purpose of this lesson is to bring the students' home culture into the classroom to build community. Therefore, getting photographs from home is optimal. Prepare and send a letter home to each student's family, providing information about the project and directions for collecting photos. Some collection options are as follows:

- upload pictures to an online repository such as Flickr or a classroom Facebook page
- send digital pictures to you via email
- send digital pictures to you on a CD or flashdrive
- send physical pictures to school so you may scan them

Some students may not have access to pictures from home, so you may take a picture of the student with a digital camera; scan a drawing by the student of family members, pets, or important events; or capture a photo from the Internet of places the student has been or experiences the student may have had.

Once the pictures have been collected, upload them to VoiceThread so students can access pictures from any computer at the same time. For this lesson, you may upload all the pictures, including your example, to one class VoiceThread.

Uploading and narrating images is easy; however, you should explore and experiment with the program by creating your own digital picture in preparation for this lesson. This will allow time to think through the many steps and strategies that you will need to model and explain to students.

Step 2: Introduce the lesson and model the process. Explain the purpose of the lesson, to learn about each other and create community, to the class. Project an image of your VoiceThread example so students have a model in mind and also because you are a member of the classroom community. Tell students they will each create a unique digital picture or story.

Navigating through an online application needs to be a strategic process, not a guessing game. First, display the main page of the VoiceThread (see Figure 3.1 for a teacher example). Model reading the information on the left side of the page but note that this information doesn't let users know how to access the VoiceThread. Emphasize that there are no directions for this.

Next, move the cursor over the information on the left. Think aloud about how you notice that when the cursor isn't hovering over the information, it appears as an arrow, but when it is hovering over the information, it turns into a hand. This means that the information is actually a link and if students click the link, it will take them to a new screen that provides more information about that topic.

The default link that is highlighted when the MyVoice page is opened is "created by me" and shows your VoiceThread on the right side of the page. Think aloud about how this link makes the most sense to click since the first photo shown on the VoiceThread is of you.

There are still no directions displayed for how to open the VoiceThread, so model moving the cursor over the VoiceThread so students can see that the arrow changes to a hand. Once the hand moves over the VoiceThread, it displays a description. Think aloud about how the description helps you to know that this is the right link to click and what will happen if you click the VoiceThread. Keep in mind that this modeling is critical: Strategically choosing what icons or links to click for more information becomes extremely important, especially as students experiment with more advanced websites that have numerous linked words, images, and icons. Once you click on the VoiceThread, the first page opens up into a larger screen (Figure 3.2).

The next step is for the students to find their own pictures. Again, this page has no directions about how to navigate through the VoiceThread. Model thinking through the different words and icons on the page to determine which one makes the most sense to click to find the other pictures in the VoiceThread. Then show how to use the arrow key to go through the pictures.

Phase 2: Teacher and student demonstrations

Now that students have observed how to think strategically about navigating to their photo, it's time to demonstrate how to write a caption and craft a message that will become the recorded narrative. Begin by telling the students that once they find their picture, it's time to type a caption and record the narrative. Again, VoiceThread doesn't provide directions for how to type or record, but the word *comment* and icon appear below the picture. When students move the cursor over the word and/or speech bubble, it changes to reveal the options to type or record a message. Next, model the process of how to type and record a message. There are several ways to record an audio message (by phone, video, or microphone on the computer). Be sure to model the strategic process of which icon to click to record.

For the remainder of this phase, model how to craft a caption and audio message that add layers of understanding to a photograph. Students have a limited knowledge of

Figure 3.1. MyVoice Page Showing One VoiceThread

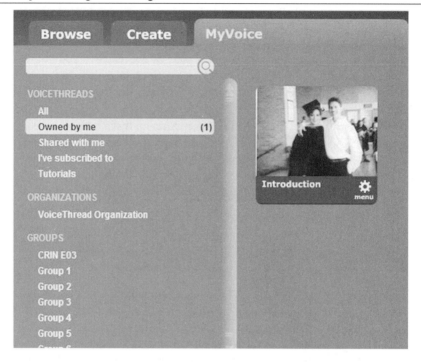

Figure 3.2. First Page of a VoiceThread

one another's lives, so the photographs in the VoiceThread have the potential to provide layers of new knowledge because multimedia images convey a wealth of information. For example, the picture in Figure 3.2 is of me, dressed in a cap and gown, with a man whose arm is around me, and we are smiling. You can infer from the cap and gown that I am graduating and the man is someone to whom I am close, probably a family member, and that we are very happy. However, a well-crafted caption could provide more information, clarifying that the man is my husband and that we are at my graduation for my doctorate degree from the University of Memphis. An audio narration would provide even more information, explaining that my immediate family had flown in from all over the United States and was waiting to surprise me with a party. My voice conveys my happiness about the surprise party in a way that a caption could not. When viewers integrate the three sources of information—photo, caption, and audio message—they have a deeper understanding than if they only had a picture. Teachers might consider modeling this process by first displaying their photograph within the VoiceThread. Ask students what information they can infer from looking at the picture. From the information the students volunteer, glean the "who, what, when, where" questions that would bring clarity to the image. The responses to these questions will be the heart of a good caption. Explain that captions are often used in nonfiction books to describe photos, illustrations, graphics, or other information that may or may not be discussed further in the text. Then, move the Voice-Thread to a student's picture and repeat the inferring process. Repeat the process once or twice with different students' photographs. Very young children may have difficulty spelling the words they want to write, but captions usually consist of words the children write often such as, "This is my mom and me at home." Captions need not be elaborate.

After modeling the inferring process with students' pictures, have students work in pairs to create their captions. Students can help one another by asking questions and synthesizing information into a brief caption. Students can also write their captions on paper and add them to VoiceThread at a later time. (This could be a stopping place if time is short.)

Next, tell students that there is more information you would like them to know about your picture. Think aloud about how you decided on the background story for your recorded narrative. Make sure students understand that you are providing different information than what is included in the caption and talk about how all three sources provide more information than one. Then select two or three individual students to discuss the background stories behind their pictures.

Finally, students work in pairs to discuss the background stories for their pictures and write them down. Consider creating a document that provides a space for each student to write the caption and narrative on one sheet of paper.

Phase 3: Independent practice

Have students work collaboratively in pairs to type the caption and record the narrative for their photographs. This can be done in one or more days. Recording the narrative is easy so students should be given the opportunity to listen to their narratives and then rerecord several times for accuracy and prosody. For young children, typing the caption may take some time. Allowing students to work collaboratively will let them support one another in the process of thinking critically about and creating the project.

Culminating activity: View the VoiceThread as a class. Engage students in discussing what they have learned about each other and how that creates a stronger learning community. Also, engage students in evaluating the digital tool used and their finished products.

Follow-up activities:

- *Respond to students' pictures.* As mentioned, one aspect of VoiceThread that makes it a rich technology is the ability to comment on people's pictures and narratives. This digital form of reader response allows students to share their thoughts and feelings about classmates. Be sure to model how to use the technology in this manner and what constitutes a thoughtful response. Set a schedule so all students have an opportunity to comment.
- *Create a chart of new understandings.* Once students have created their individual VoiceThreads and responded to other's VoiceThreads, they have learned a great deal about their classmates including commonalities and differences. Creating a chart of new understandings enables students to see how that information is important to building classroom community. Using chart paper or an online graphing program (such as Create A Graph available at: nces.ed.gov/nceskids/createagraph/default.aspx), have students discuss the different activities that they like to do, places they have visited, people that are important in their lives, and so forth (see Figure 3.3 for an example) to determine how much students have in common.
- *Connect with families.* Allow family members access to the VoiceThreads. In a letter to parents, provide the link and ask each family to comment on their child's VoiceThread and optionally, other students' VoiceThreads. Alternately, post a link to the class VoiceThread with instructions on commenting to the class website, Facebook page, blog, or send this information via email.

IRT LESSON FOR OLDER STUDENTS: DIGITAL STORYTELLING

This lesson builds on the same understandings for using VoiceThread that are necessary for younger students but involves several pictures, captions, and narratives that come together in a brief memoir for each student. When older students understand the basic components of VoiceThread, they will be ready for more in-depth use of the program. A key concept for students to understand is the layer of knowledge that is developed *within* each photo, caption, and narrative and the multiple layers of understanding that will develop *across* the VoiceThread as a whole.

Phase 1: Teacher modeling

Step 1: Planning the lesson. You will need to:

- choose what digital storytelling program to use
- decide on the time frame and number of photographs each student should bring

Figure 3.3. Graph Created from Class VoiceThread Depicting How Much Students Have in Common

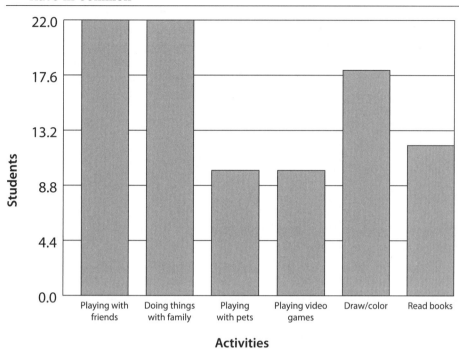

- determine how to collect photographs
- create your own storyboard/VoiceThread memoir example
- decide which strategies your students will need to navigate through the program

The aforementioned planning steps, with the exception of the time frame and number of photographs, mirror those discussed in the IRT for younger students. For a VoiceThread memoir, decide on the time frame within which students are to work (e.g., birth to present day or kindergarten to present day). Then decide on the number of photos students can use to capture those years; between five and eight usually work well. Since students will have several pictures, decide if you or students will upload them. If you upload the pictures, then students will need to provide you with the order of the photos prior to the lesson. If the students populate their own VoiceThread, then you will need to model how to do this.

Step 2: Introduce the lesson and model the process. Explain the purpose of the lesson is for students to get to know each other and build community. Share your own VoiceThread memoir.

To model the strategic process of using the VoiceThread and finding students' photographs, follow the directions for the IRT lesson for younger students. Modify the IRT lesson as necessary to reflect the strategic needs of your students. For example, you may not need to do as much, if any, modeling of how to navigate within VoiceThread.

Phase 2: Teacher and student demonstrations

Since students will include several photos in their VoiceThread memoirs, they first need to determine the order of the photos, then create the captions and narratives. A graphic organizer, such as the storyboard in Figure 3.4, can provide a way for students to plan the order of their photos and to craft captions and narration. After showing students your VoiceThread memoir, show them your storyboard and think aloud about your decisionmaking process for ordering your pictures and creating captions and narration.

Creating captions provides an opportunity to show students the importance of the wording in writing. Show students a picture from a nonfiction trade book or textbook and ask what they can see in the picture. Then share the caption and discuss. How were students' observations similar to the caption? Different? Also, note that once a topic or subject has been introduced, it usually isn't introduced or labeled again in subsequent photos. Therefore, if a student has several pictures of parents, siblings, or a family pet for example, they need to be introduced only on first mention and then referred to by name thereafter.

For creating the audio narratives, discuss the need for adding information that elaborates on and extends the caption. Also, discuss creating transitions between photos so the VoiceThread truly represents a memoir rather than a disjointed collection of photos.

Have students work in pairs to collaborate on their storyboards. In this way, they can share ideas for crafting captions and providing details for narration. After students have created their storyboards, select two or three to demonstrate to the class.

To model how to type captions and record narratives in VoiceThread, follow the directions for the IRT lesson for younger students.

Figure 3.4. Graphic Organizer for Planning a VoiceThread Memoir

PHOTO 1	**PHOTO 2**
Caption: Narration:	Caption: Narration:
PHOTO 3	**PHOTO 4**
Caption: Narration:	Caption: Narration:

Phase 3: Independent practice

Have students work independently to type the captions and record the narratives for their memoirs. This can be done in one or more days.

Culminating activity: Show two or three students' VoiceThread memoirs each day until the class has viewed them all. Engage students in discussion and reflection on what they have learned about each other and how that makes their community stronger. Also, engage students in evaluating the digital tool used to create their memoirs and the evaluation of their own products.

Follow-up activities:

- **Document friendships, learning experiences, and more.** As the year progresses, students can add class photos to VoiceThread that depict students' engaged in new friendships, field trips, science experiments, or numerous other activities. Students may also add photos taken at home that document important events in their lives or something they want to share.
- **Document learning in various subjects.** Digital storytelling has a variety of uses that students can use to document learning in various subjects (e.g., to write or retell a story, research in a content area, document the steps taken in a scientific experiment, or to study cultures).

King or Queen for the Day

King or Queen for the Day (Cunningham, 2008) is an activity that helps children get to know one another at the beginning of the year. At the beginning of each day, select a different student to be king or queen for the day. Often, the child wears a special crown and sits in a special chair in front of the class. Once you select the king or queen, ask the student a series of questions that allows the class to get to know the king or queen's interests and life outside of school.

For younger students, it is helpful if these questions are displayed and follow a pattern such as, "The Queen for the Day is ——— She likes to eat . . . . She likes to play . . . . She has . . . sister(s) and . . . brother(s)." Use presentation software such as PowerPoint or a blank Word or Google document to type the king or queen's responses to the patterned sentences that are displayed for the class to see. Younger children can then identify known letters or words in the sentences, and the student's name can become part of the word wall. English language learners and bilingual students can share their interests in the words of their home language. For example, if a child's favorite food is spaghetti and his or her home language is Spanish, the sentence could read, "He (or she) likes to eat spaghetti (espaguetis)."

Take a picture of the king or queen wearing the crown and sitting in the special chair. Insert the picture into the slide or document. Print the page for the child to take home and have the other students draw a picture of the king or queen and write something they learned about him or her on the paper. Then scan the printed page and the students' drawings into a book that each child can take home or that you place in the classroom library.

With some tweaking, this activity is also a great way for older students to get to know one another. Rather than select a king or queen for the day, you might designate a class leader (or another title) for the day. Older students could type their own messages regarding the leader, and, rather than drawing a picture, the students could write letters indicating something they learned from the message or something they have in common with the leader.

Once the entire class has had the opportunity to be the king or queen or the leader, then the daily routine can become the morning message in which the class leader contributes news or a comment. Teachers or students may post these messages to a class website, wiki, blog, Facebook page, or other site so students and families may view and comment.

Blogging

Given their interactive nature, blogs provide unique opportunities for creating classroom community, allowing students to create content in ways not possible with a traditional journal. Students can read and respond to one another's posts, and this shift in audience—from the teacher to the class, and even to an audience outside the classroom—fundamentally changes students' motivation and engagement with writing (Weiser, Fehler, & Gonzalez, 2009).

Creating blogs is free, safe, and easy. Online providers such as Kidblog, Blogger, and Edublogs provide individual student accounts with privacy settings that dictate whom may access the blog. Once you have created and modeled how to use student blogs, ask students to use their blogs at the end of the school day to reflect on their daily learning. Then, have students read and respond to one another's posts, but be sure to model how to comment on a blog first (see Chapter 7 for more on blogs). As students engage in this activity, they may find that they have common interests, add to one another's understanding of daily learning activities, or share resources such as useful websites, images, or applications. You can also read and respond to students' blogs, as can family members if they have access.

As the year progresses, students can link and connect to other blogs and ideas from other online resources. For example, when students respond in writing to a book or poem, their responses could include links and connections to another student's blog. Students may also include links to external websites (e.g., an author's blog or website, and a book reviewer's blog). To make these connections and communicate them in writing, however, students must engage in close reading and reflection, think critically within and across sources of information, and form a clear, concise message for a real audience. For an example of a classroom blog, visit yollisclassblog.blogspot.com.

CREATING COMMUNITY WITH FAMILIES AND THE LARGER COMMUNITY

Ferguson, Jordan, and Baldwin (2010) found that teacher outreach to parents was related to strong and consistent gains in student performance in both reading and math, making it clear that "When schools build partnerships with families that respond to their concerns and honor their contributions, they are successful in sustaining connections that are aimed at improving student achievement" (p. 1). If families are to be partners in their children's education, schools and teachers must engage them in practices that focus on building trusting, collaborative relationships that recognize and respect families' needs, as well as their cultural differences. The technology-focused, classroom community-building activities in this chapter represent just one approach that:

- includes families in decisionmaking about their child's experience that is expected, welcomed, and supported
- engages families in consistent, two-way, and linguistically and culturally appropriate communication
- embraces families' knowledge, skills, and backgrounds and integrates them into children's learning experiences
- helps families develop home environments that enhance learning

What about families who don't have Internet access? For families that do not have access to the Internet, the following are a few ways to communicate and share their children's projects:

- Ask families the best way to communicate with them. It may be that they have a cell phone or they have email access at work, and pictures or projects can be sent to the phone or email.
- Videotape the child's presentation and send it home for parents to view.
- Invite families to come to school to see their child's project.
- Projects can be printed and sent home with a personalized note.

Regardless of the form of communication, families should be encouraged to provide feedback on their child's project. Given the opportunity to take part in welcoming projects that value them, families become more connected to their children, the classroom, and the school. The online projects described in this chapter and throughout this book create a nurturing classroom community and assist families in gaining confidence in their contributions to their children's education.

CHAPTER 4

Vocabulary and Fluency

An individual's knowledge of words is made up of both general terms used in everyday language and academic terms used in specialized subjects such as math and science. Everyone's vocabulary knowledge is unique, based on background knowledge, experiences with books, and parents' vocabulary level. Students from high socioeconomic (SES) homes typically have a vocabulary greater than those from low SES homes (Beck, McKeown, & Kucan, 2002). Moreover, children from high SES homes grow their vocabularies at a faster pace. Estimates indicate that the average child from a high SES home entering kindergarten has a vocabulary of approximately 3,500 words and the average graduate from a high SES high school has a reading vocabulary of between 40,000 and 50,000 words (Baker, Simmons, & Kame'enui, 1998). Thus, high SES students learn about 3,000 words per school year; however, students from low SES homes learn more slowly than their high SES counterparts. Students who reach 4th grade with limited vocabularies are very likely to struggle to understand grade-level texts (Chall & Jacobs, 2003; RAND Study Group, 2002).

Numerous studies have documented that vocabulary knowledge is highly predictive of reading comprehension (Baker, Simmons, & Kame'enui, 1998; Beck, Perfetti, & McKeown, 1982; Cunningham & Stanovich, 1997). The more words readers know, the better they will be able to understand what they read. In a review of 100 years of vocabulary research, Graves and Watts-Taffe (2002) made the following findings:

- One of the best indicators of verbal ability is vocabulary knowledge.
- The difficulty of the vocabulary in a text strongly influences the readability of the text.
- Vocabulary instruction can improve students' comprehension.
- Growing up in poverty can seriously restrict vocabulary acquisition before children begin school, and challenges vocabulary retention. Less advantaged students are likely to have substantially smaller vocabularies than their more advantaged classmates.
- Lack of vocabulary can be a critical factor underlying the school failure of disadvantaged students.

Graves and Watts-Taffe (2002) conclude by revealing what is arguably the most important factor to consider in planning vocabulary instruction: "The task of learning vocabulary is a huge task" (p. 141). It is also critical—too critical to leave to chance. This chapter will discuss ways technology can enhance vocabulary instruction to support student comprehension.

ACTIVITIES FOR VOCABULARY INSTRUCTION

What do you think when you read the word *sandwich*? Do you think of two slices of bread with fillings and condiments between them? Or does a picture of your favorite sandwich pop into your mind? More than likely, it was the latter. Cunningham and Allington (2011) write:

> When we see or hear words, our brains make all kinds of connections with those words, depending on our past experiences. These connections include images and scenes from our own lives as well as from movies and television. We have emotional reactions to words. Words make us worry, celebrate, appreciate, and wonder. What our minds don't do when they see or hear a word is think of a definition. (p. 95)

Research has shown that readers process and remember new information more effectively when they actively receive language through both expressive and receptive modes (reading information and listening to and viewing information), particularly when faced with high comprehension demands. When information is simultaneously presented and processed through both modes of communication, the brain will make connections between the two, which strengthens readers' ability to learn and remember new information (Clark & Paivio, 1991). To evoke an image and an emotional reaction, a word must be fully known, which requires much more than a dictionary definition. According to Beck, McKeown, and Kucan (2002), knowledge of a word follows a continuum:

- no knowledge—the word is completely unknown
- incidental knowledge—the word may have been seen before but is unknown
- partial knowledge—one definition of the word is known or it can be used in only one context
- full knowledge—multiple meanings of the word are known and can be used appropriately in multiple contexts

Full understanding of a word requires multiple opportunities to use and think about the word's meanings in multiple contexts. Multimedia can provide these multiple contexts. Research on the use of short video clips to provide a context for learning found this approach to vocabulary instruction especially supportive for English language learners (ELLs). Multimedia to support vocabulary learning can be used during direct instruction and when reading independently. Many online interactive storybooks such as those discussed in Chapter 5, include built-in mediation and support for vocabulary. Blachowicz, Fisher, Ogle, and Watts-Taffe (2006) found that "electronic texts can be both motivating and effective for word learning when they provide or couple their presentations with facilitation that calls on the students to actively engage with the words" (p. 533).

Students typically have opportunities to learn vocabulary throughout the day—when teachers read aloud to students, when teachers and students read shared texts together, when teachers assist students during small group reading, and when students read independently. The reciprocal process is true when writing throughout the day, which is discussed in Chapter 7. Online resources can enrich these word-learning opportunities.

Reading Aloud: Using Multimedia to Support Vocabulary Instruction

Reading aloud can be an effective way to develop word knowledge if the books present more sophisticated vocabulary and concepts than are in students' existing vocabularies. However, vocabulary instruction based on read-alouds must be intentional, since students with smaller initial vocabularies are less likely than students with larger vocabularies to learn vocabulary incidentally. Therefore, younger students need a thoughtful, well-designed, scaffolded approach to maximize learning from picture book read-alouds. Important characteristics of effective scaffolded instruction (Blachowicz, Fisher, Ogle, & Watts-Taffe, 2006) are as follows:

- present students with an explanation of the words that will make sense to them
- engage students in activating their prior knowledge and integrating it with new information, as well as building connections to related categories of words and concepts
- design meaningful activities for engaging students in using the words in a variety of contexts
- develop assessments that gauge students' depth of knowledge about the words

Combining the traditional read-aloud format with video that reinforces the meaning of the text may benefit students, especially struggling readers and ELLs (Verhallen, Bus, & de Jong, 2006). Video may provide students with more robust receptive information than the static illustrations in picture books and allow them to more effectively use their receptive processing system to support their expressive processing of the picturebook content (Silverman & Hines, 2009). However, it's important that students, especially struggling readers and ELLs, understand how to integrate knowledge from two media sources into their prior knowledge. This chapter's IRT lesson for younger students shows how to scaffold this type of processing.

Often, reading aloud stops in the primary grades, but reading aloud is just as important for older students. Many sophisticated picture books provide insight, information, and perspective on almost any curriculum topic. For example, *When Marian Sang: The True Recital of Marian Anderson* (Ryan, 2002) is a wonderful picture book rich with robust vocabulary about the great singer. Her historic 1939 concert at the Lincoln Memorial drew an integrated audience of over 75,000 during a time of segregation. Several brief videos of Anderson singing at the concert, available on YouTube, bring to life many of the robust vocabulary words used in the book, such as *unwavering, trepidation*, and *awe*, and provide an extended context for learning the meaning of these words.

IRT LESSON FOR YOUNGER STUDENTS: READ-ALOUDS

Phase 1: Teacher modeling

Step 1: Planning the lesson. You will need to decide:

- which picture book to read
- which vocabulary words to highlight
- what word learning strategies to model
- what video to use to enrich the vocabulary from the read aloud

This IRT lesson will use video to support vocabulary instruction from a picture book read-aloud. Thus, in this lesson, the teacher will model how to integrate information from video (receptive processing) with information learned during the read-aloud (expressive processing) and reassemble into existing prior knowledge.

First select the picture book to read aloud. For this lesson, you may consider using *Time to Sleep* (Fleming, 1997). In this fictional tale the author uses rich vocabulary to describe the actions of the animals as they prepare to hibernate during winter. In addition, the author has written other science related books that use rich vocabulary such as *Beetle Bop* (Fleming, 2007); *In the Small, Small Pond* (Fleming, 1993); *Lunch* (Fleming, 1992); and *In the Tall, Tall Grass* (Fleming, 1991). *Time to Sleep* could be part of an author study in which students learn why Denise Fleming likes to write about animals and bugs and about her writing style.

The next step is to decide which vocabulary words should be taught. As a general rule, words that are frequently used in written texts, have high utility, and are most likely to enter students' reading, writing, listening, and speaking vocabularies are most worth highlighting and teaching to elementary students. Keep in mind that without direct instruction, students may not learn. Using these criteria can be very helpful in selecting words to teach across learning contexts. The key word in *Time to Sleep* is *hibernate*, though the word is not specifically used in the book. However, this lends itself to a very nice deductive book introduction, which will be discussed in the following section. Other words such as *slithering, rumbled, ramble, trudged, burrow, perched,* and *grumbled* are excellent for drawing attention to precise word choice in writing.

The video selected should be brief and extend students' understanding of the vocabulary terms into new contexts. For this lesson, the video, Hibernating Animals by *Time for Kids* (www.timeforkids.com/photos-video/video/hibernating-animals-24476), extends the students' contextual knowledge of animals that hibernate by providing photos of and information about hibernating animals not included in the book. (The education section of YouTube offers many videos to support vocabulary instruction.) So, students' contextual knowledge of *hibernate* is expanded by moving from fiction to the real world, and by increasing knowledge of the number of animals that hibernate and the contexts and conditions in which these animals hibernate. Be sure to scaffold students' engagement with the video by discussing words in the context of the video.

Step 2: Introduce the lesson. Introduce the book. Point to the bear on the front cover and make the point that animals need to sleep just like humans. However, unlike humans, some animals, like this bear, sleep through the winter.

Activate prior knowledge by asking if anyone knows what it is called when animals sleep through the winter. In this way, you can assess how many students have some understanding of hibernation.

Explicitly state the definition of hibernate, write the word where all students can see it, and ask students to say the word with you. Then state that the purpose of reading *Time to Sleep* is to find out some of the different animals that hibernate in the winter.

Read the story. Stop reading to draw attention to the words (precise word choice) used to describe the animals and their actions. For example, the first page reads, "Bear sniffed once. She sniffed twice. 'I smell winter in the air,' said Bear." Ask students to *show* you what *sniffed* means. Then, ask if anyone can tell you what clues the author provided for figuring out what the word means (e.g., close-up illustration of bear's nose in the air and definition of *sniffed* following its use). Finally, ask why the author didn't use another word like *breathed*? (Perhaps *breathed* doesn't describe what the bear is doing as well as *sniffed*.) All these activities help students become conscious of the importance word choice plays in conveying a message.

As you read, make connections by stopping to discuss whether students may find any of the animals in the surrounding neighborhoods where the students live.

Finally, engage all students in actively processing new learning. After finishing the story, ask students to turn to a partner, define *hibernate*, and list some of the animals that hibernate in the story. Then, call on several students to share this information with the whole class.

Step 3: Model the process. Complete this step immediately following the read-aloud or the next day.

Tell the students they are going to watch a short video about animals that hibernate. Then guide them to notice new information in the video—seeing new animals that hibernate and hearing new words such as *nocturnal* and *venom*.

Draw students' attention to inflectional endings. Under the word *hibernate* originally displayed where all students could see and say it at the beginning of the read-aloud, write the different forms of *hibernate* used in the video: *hibernate, hibernates, hibernation*. Point out that these are all forms of *hibernate*.

Activate background knowledge by asking students to think about what they learned from *Time to Sleep* (Fleming, 1997) as they watch the video.

Finally, play the video. Then explain to students that you are going to replay the video immediately, stopping at certain points to show how the animals hibernate. Replay the video to each stopping point and discuss how each animal hibernates.

Phase 2: Teacher and student demonstrations

Model integrating new information from the video with information learned from the book. An example follows:

As I watched the video, I thought about what I knew from the book. For example, in the book, Bear tells Snail, "It is time to seal your shell and sleep." So, I learned from the book that when snails hibernate, they seal their shell. The video told me that snails seal their shells, but it also told me that the reason is so the snail will stay moist. The book showed a picture of only one snail, but the video told me that snails group together during hibernation and showed a picture of lots of snails together on a log.

Reiterate why it is important for students to be able to integrate information from multiple sources, and then call on one or more students to share how they integrated information from the book with what they learned from the video.

Phase 3: Independent practice

Engage all students in actively processing new information learned in the video by asking students to work with a partner to discuss the new animals they learned about in the video and how they hibernate. Alternately, engage students in an activity in which they must decide if an animal hibernates or not. Tell students that you are going to list different animals and, if any of the animals hibernate, they are to say "hibernate" and if not, don't say anything.

Provide an opportunity for each student to draw a picture of an animal hibernating from the book or the video and write the word *hibernate* under the picture. Students could also add the word *hibernate* to their vocabulary notebook, online flashcards, or create a podcast (discussed below).

IRT LESSON FOR OLDER STUDENTS: READ-ALOUDS

Phase 1: Teacher modeling

Step 1: Planning the lesson. You will need to decide:

- which online learning resource to read aloud
- which vocabulary words to highlight
- what word learning strategies to model
- what strategies to model for integrating multimedia

The IRT lesson for older students moves from learning to integrate information from traditional print with video to learning to integrate information from multiple online sources. As discussed, most students use online networks to extend friendships rather than explore interests or find information beyond what they have access to at school or in their community (Ito et al., 2008). This lack of engagement with online networks as a learning resource presents an opportunity to assist students in learning how to make the most of online learning. This involves learning to integrate information from multiple online sources, which may include a variety of multimedia.

First, decide which online learning resource to use. Online news specifically geared toward kids is a great resource, since it usually includes content-specific vocabulary, along with graphics and video clips. Many quality online resources are available, such as:

- Scholastic News (K–6, www.scholastic.com)
- Time for Kids (K–6, www.timeforkids.com)
- Weekly Reader (3–6, www.weeklyreader.com/subcategory/74)
- Dogonews (3–6, www.dogonews.com)
- CNN Student News (6–12, www.cnn.com/studentnews)
- Tween Tribune (K–12, www.tweentribune.com)
- Youngzine (K–12, www.youngzine.org)

Children today tend to learn news of their neighborhood, the nation, and the world by absorbing information from parents and other family members. Few pick up a daily newspaper or weekly newsmagazine. Some may click on a news story or video of a news story when friends post links on Facebook. For the most part, however, students' engagement with news tends to be rare and fleeting.

The next step is to decide on the vocabulary you will highlight—the selection process will be similar to the process for the IRT lesson for younger students—and the strategies you will need to model for figuring out these words in the text. Some online resources may link specific words to additional information. This leads to the next question: What strategies are needed to model the integration of this information into prior vocabulary knowledge? It also provides an opportunity to model how to determine whether linked information is helpful.

This specific lesson is based on the online learning resource Wonderopolis (wonderopolis.org), which is sponsored by the National Center for Family Literacy (NCFL). Wonderopolis provides a different question or wonder, every day, to spark curiosity. Each wonder follows the same format. The opening webpage displays the question, which is accompanied by a photo that provides insight into the answer. Often, the question leads to the exploration of a science or social studies topic, and usually involves a particular vocabulary word; however, the site also highlights idioms or other uses of language that may be unique. For example, the wonder used in this IRT lesson focuses on *funny bone*, which is not only a nickname for the ulnar nerve that runs along the inside part of the elbow but an idiom (e.g., when something "tickles your funny bone").

As discussed, clicking on the aforementioned photo will take you to a second page with additional information. This page provides the following:

- a 2-minute (or less) video clip in response to the question
- additional questions to explore the topic (Have you ever wondered . . . ?)
- information that answers the question (Did you know?)
- follow-up activities to learn more about the topic (Try It Out)
- additional vocabulary related to the topic (Wonder Words)
- an extension activity (Still Wondering)

The investigation of words through Wonderopolis activities increases students' awareness, appreciation, motivation, and interest in words.

Step 2: Introduce the lesson. Introduce the online resource. This may seem simple, but modeling engagement with online networks as a learning resource is an important first step. Let students know they will be using Wonderopolis specifically to learn the following:

- how to use the Internet as an important source of information for everyone
- how to find trustworthy sites
- how to read, view, and navigate online resources effectively

State the purpose of the site (i.e., Wonderopolis makes learning fun and interesting). Then display the first page of the Wonder of the Day (see Figure 4.1), making sure to discuss the site's structure, since understanding the structure will facilitate comprehension. The Wonderopolis site presents a question along with a supporting image. Explain that students should make their best guess based on their prior knowledge and the image. Also explain that once students click on the image, more information is provided to assist in answering the question.

Step 3: Model the process. Read aloud the title of the page (Figure 4.1) and activate prior knowledge: What do students already know about the funny bone? Then allow students to share their prior knowledge.

Figure 4.1. First Page of Wonderopolis Wonder of the Day with Image and Question of the Day

Source: Wonderopolis is brought to life by the National Center for Family Literacy. Material available at wonderopolis.org/tag/bone/

Model how to integrate information from the image. Think aloud about what you see and how that connects to your prior knowledge of the topic. The image of a smiling skeleton seems to suggest that a funny bone is a bone in a person's body that can make them laugh, but it also seems to personify the term *funny bone* with the smiling skeleton. This image doesn't really help to answer the question, Does everyone have a funny bone? So explain to students that you need to read on (or click the photo) for more information.

After clicking on the photo, you arrive at a second page with additional information, including a video (see Figure 4.2). The 8-second video depicts an upset little girl, who cries: "It's not a funny bone, it's not. And why do you call it a funny bone?" The caption under the video reads, "Bumping into today's Wonder of the Day isn't as humerus as it might sound!" Model strategies for integrating the video into prior knowledge. Think aloud about how this new information fits with your previous thoughts about the smiling skeleton image. The little girl is crying, and her comment indicates that a funny bone isn't funny. The video and caption confirm that a funny bone isn't a bone that makes people laugh. Plus, there is an additional piece of information from the incorrect spelling of humorous (i.e., *humerus*). Explain that the information from the video has changed your thinking—now you think *funny bone* is a play on words, just as the use of *humerus* is a play on words—so you will read on to find out what the funny bone really is.

Read aloud to confirm or revise predictions based on multiple media sources, stopping to model how to figure out unknown vocabulary. The "Did you know?" section on Wonderopolis begins, "Everyone loves to laugh. Whether it's because of a funny movie, a good knock-knock joke[hyperlink] or a clown, smiling and laughing just make us feel better." After reading this sentence aloud, discuss with students why this information doesn't help with answering the question.

Model strategies for figuring out unfamiliar vocabulary. Also discuss the term *knock-knock joke*, which on the page is a link, as indicated by its different color and change in the cursor (from an arrow to a hand) when hovering over the term. Discuss why you would not choose to click on this link, since it would not help you answer the question, "Does everyone have a funny bone?"

Phase 2: Teacher and student demonstrations

Release responsibility for using strategies to students. Select a short section of text for students to read independently:

> If you've ever hit your <u>funny bone</u>[hyperlink], you probably remember it. If you bump the inside of your elbow in just that certain place, you'll experience a weird tingling feeling or maybe even a dull pain that smarts just a bit. It usually feels like a weird "pins and needles" sensation and it may hurt.

Then, ask them to discuss with a partner how the section adds to their understanding of the text and whether there was any unfamiliar vocabulary. Ask one or more students to share their process and the strategies they used to figure out unfamiliar vocabulary. In this selection, *funny bone* provided a link to additional information. Did

Figure 4.2. Second Page of Wonderopolis Wonder of the Day with Video

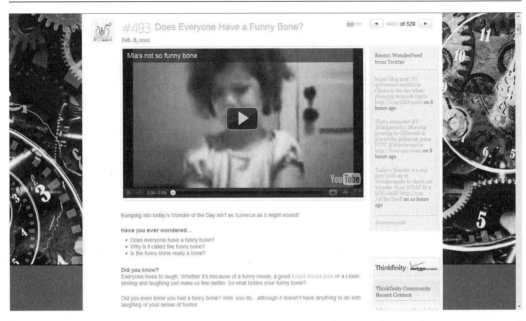

Source: Wonderopolis is brought to life by the National Center for Family Literacy. Material available at wonderopolis.org/wonder/does-everyone-have-a-funny-bone/

students click on this link? Why? Why not? Repeat this process with at least one more section of text.

Phase 3: Independent practice

Ask student to finish reading the text independently using the strategies discussed previously. When students are finished, discuss the overall response to the text and the strategies students used to figure out unknown words or whether to click on links.

Follow-up activities:

- ***Craft and post a class response to the reading.*** Wonderopolis and other online learning resources allow readers to comment. This is a great way to teach students appropriate ways to respond online. Reading through a few existing responses with students allows them to see what others thought about the reading.
- ***Create an online learning resource.*** The Wonderopolis site follows the same structure for each wonder posted, so students could easily follow this structure to create and post their own wonders online. This activity provides an opportunity to discuss the reciprocal process of choosing a supportive image, video and linked words, and terms or phrases.

Independent Reading

Wide reading is one of the most widely acknowledged (and incidental) ways of building students' general word knowledge. Nagy (1988) states:

> Most growth in vocabulary knowledge must necessarily come through reading. There is no way that vocabulary instruction alone can provide students with enough experiences with enough words to produce both the depth and breadth of vocabulary knowledge that they need to attain. Increasing the volume of students' reading is the single most important thing a teacher can do to promote large-scale vocabulary growth. (p. 32)

When reading independently, children should encounter rich vocabulary in contexts provided by authentic texts. Good literature can take children places that classroom experiences cannot, such as Narnia in *The Lion, the Witch, and the Wardrobe* (Lewis, 1950), Nazi-occupied Denmark during the Holocaust in *Number the Stars* (Lowry, 1989), or the world of arachnids in *Amazing Spiders* (Parsons, 1990). These vicarious experiences provide a powerful way to learn word meanings. While reading independently, students can self-select vocabulary words they want to study.

Self-selected vocabulary. When students have choice in what they learn and what they read, it makes a difference. For example, allowing students the freedom to choose their own books for independent reading has been shown to increase motivation (Edmonds & Bauserman, 2006; Ivey & Johnston, 2013). Similarly, letting students select what words to learn has been shown to increase word knowledge and use of this knowledge in writing, motivation, and study skills (Fisher, Blachowicz, & Smith, 1991; McCarthy, 1990; Walters & Bozkurt, 2009).

Literature is a rich source of vocabulary, providing students with a means to mine words and bring them to the surface. While reading independently, students can write words that are new, interesting, or unusual. Initially, students can use a think mark (Baumann, Ware, & Edwards, 2007) to write words quickly without interrupting sustained reading time. Students use think marks as they would a bookmark; however, think marks provide space to list the book title and genre, and new, interesting, or unusual words. Encourage students to include three to four new words a week from a variety of genres. Then have them discuss the words during small group instruction, literature discussion groups, and word study activities.

As an extension activity, students may illustrate, define, and use these words in a sentence in their vocabulary notebooks. Creating an online vocabulary notebook enriches vocabulary learning opportunities for students in several ways. First, students may continue their learning when they are away from school since the notebooks are available anywhere and anytime. Second, students may add music, videos, and scanned illustrations of words to their notebooks to add additional contexts and layers of meaning to their vocabulary knowledge. Finally, students may record themselves reading the words and definitions aloud, which reinforces word knowledge and provides fluency practice.

Presentation software is a great tool for creating vocabulary notebooks (see Figure 4.3), which you or students may then save and post on students' blogs, classroom wiki, or classroom website. Students may also create vocabulary notebooks in Google docs or directly on their blogs.

Content-Area Reading

Often, general vocabulary and word identification strategies are the main emphasis in the primary grades, but as students progress into more difficult content-area reading, words are labels for concepts that can only be acquired through repeated exposure in a variety of meaningful contexts. For example, a student who encounters the word *photosynthesis* in a science textbook may be able to use word identification strategies to figure out the pronunciation, but may not understand the meaning if it is not explicitly stated in the text or revealed through context clues. This type of specialized vocabulary, which is particularly challenging for ELLs, goes beyond students' experiences, as Nagy and Townsend (2012) note:

Students in K–12 settings with limited academic language proficiency will not come to understand words like *structure* or *function* by memorizing definitions. Rather, it is re-

Figure 4.3. Slides from a Vocabulary Notebook Created in PowerPoint with Voice Narration

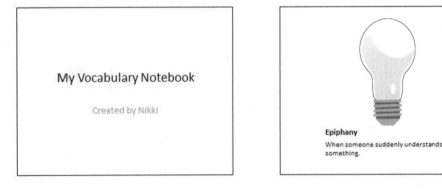

peated exposures to these words and opportunities to practice using them in authentic contexts that allow students to own these words and use them with facility in the contexts in which they both garner and support meaning of technical for theoretical ideas. (p. 96)

Specialized vocabulary requires direct instruction for students to acquire strategies for independent vocabulary acquisition. Technology—in the form of visual displays, graphic organizers, and virtual field trips—can help scaffold students' understanding of specialized vocabulary.

Visual displays of word relationships. Vocabulary learning must occur in authentic contexts, with many opportunities to learn how words interact with, get meaning from, and support meanings of other words (Nagy & Townsend, 2012). Graphic organizers and visual displays highlight the connections between words and concepts. Two free online visual display tools that support word associations are Wordle and Wordsift. Wordle (www.wordle.net) quickly allows the reader to identify the important words that appear in the text. Paste text from any document into the application, and the most important words— based on frequency of use in the text—appear larger than the other words. Wordsift (www.wordsift.com) has this feature and more. Figure 4.4 depicts a Wordsift example that is based on a chapter about cells from a 5th-grade science book. The top of the page displays a word cloud based on the text. The most important words, *cell* and *organism*, jump out at the reader. A word cloud is a great tool for previewing a chapter before students read it. Ask students to use the word cloud to determine the chapter topic and think about the relationship between the words *cell* and *organism*. (Note: students may save the word cloud from either Wordle or Wordsift as an image and include it in their online vocabulary notebooks or blogs or on the class website.)

Wordsift also provides a visual thesaurus (Figure 4.4, right side of the page), so the main word *cell* from the word cloud is displayed along with a web of its associated meanings. (Clicking on any word in the word cloud will prompt its display in the visual thesaurus.) Click on any word in the visual thesaurus to see its definition. This unique feature allows students to see common definitions of *cell* with which they are probably more familiar, such as *cell phone* and *jail cell*. It also provides a great opportunity to discuss how the word *cell* in the associated words is related to the meaning of *cell* in the chapter. Below the visual thesaurus is a listing of the sentences from the original text that was cut and pasted into the application that uses the main word that can be used as a reference if students want to find a specific instance of the word in the text.

Wordsift also includes Google search results for images and videos of the main word (or any word that is clicked) in the word cloud (Figure 4.4, left side of page). This provides multiple contexts for learning. Research has shown that the combination of explicit vocabulary instruction and videos, graphic organizers, and purposeful discussion has significant positive effects on students' vocabulary acquisition (Vaughn et al., 2009). Wordsift provides videos and graphic organizers to support direct instruction and purposeful discussion.

Virtual field trips. Another way to provide background knowledge and additional contexts for learning academic vocabulary is by taking students on field trips that

Figure 4.4. Wordsift from a 5th-Grade Science Textbook Chapter on Cells

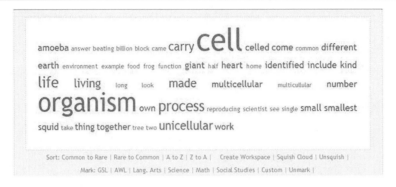

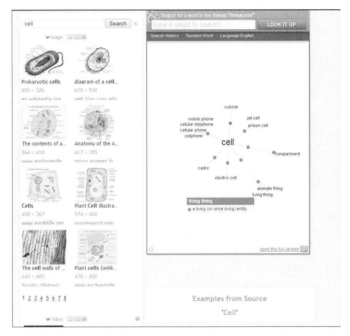

enhance curriculum content and introduce art, artifacts, and cultural resources. Lack of time and money—and, in some cases, the location of the destination—often makes field trips impossible; however, these barriers disappear with virtual field trips (VFTs). In fact, even more possibilities open up. An undersea adventure? Impossible in real time but possible in virtual time!

Several types of VFTs are as follows:

- pre-existing—have already been created and are available any time for anyone to visit
- interactive—offer experiences that take place in real-time between the students and an educator or organization
- teacher developed—are created by the teacher using personal images, videos, or websites

Pre-existing VFTs are websites—usually created by educators and organizations—that include text, images, audio, and/or video resources about specific topics. For example, the Smithsonian National Museum of Natural History offers many virtual exhibits. One exhibit allows students to explore 3D models of dinosaurs from the museum's collections and learn how fossils are discovered, unearthed, and preserved. A panoramic camera provides a 360-degree view of the dinosaur skeletons in the museum (see Figure 4.5). It's *almost* like you're there.

It is important to preview these sites in advance of curriculum planning, since some may move or shut down unexpectedly or require large amounts of bandwidth to access. E-Field Trips (www.efieldtrips.org) and Access Excellence Resource Center (www.accessexcellence.org/RC/virtual.php) provide extensive lists of pre-existing VFTs.

Interactive VFTs take place in real time via video conferencing in which students in one location learn from educators or organizations in another location. This type of videoconference isn't the same as a videoconference via an application such as Skype, which accesses the computer's webcam. Videoconferencing equipment uses a codec or computer program that shrinks large files and makes them playable on your computer, which allows the full effect of a personal experience with a large group of students. Approximately 30% of U.S. schools have this equipment (Greenberg, 2009), so check with your school before dismissing this option.

Interactive VFTs have many benefits for students. According to Zanetis (2010), "First, the medium itself enchants and engages. To be able to view, hear, and interact with people who are far away is powerful, especially if those people are articulate and

Figure 4.5. Panoramic View of Dinosaurs at the Smithsonian National Museum of Natural History

Credit line: Courtesy of Smithsonian Institution.

experts on the topic the students are studying" (p. 22). If you were a 5th-grade teacher studying cell biology with students, as described in the previous section, imagine interacting with an astronaut and discussing changes to the human body caused by living in space. NASA's Digital Learning Network (www.nasa.gov/offices/education/programs/national/dln/index.html) offers many well-designed VFTs, one of which is Humans in Space. Students would experience a unique opportunity to see, hear and interact with an astronaut at the NASA space center. For quality VFTs, check out the Center for Interactive Learning and Collaboration (www.cilc.org) and its award-winning VFT content providers (wfuedtech.weebly.com/uploads/8/5/0/1/8501459/vft.pdf).

Keep in mind, teachers may also create their own VFTs. Sarah Vetell, a 3rd-grade teacher, went to Egypt on her summer vacation. The study of Egypt is also part of her 3rd-grade social studies curriculum. Upon her return, Sarah created a VFT using the photos and video she took on the trip. She created a blog, posted the content, and used audio to narrate the site, making sure to integrate the appropriate social studies vocabulary terms. Sarah's students were thrilled not only to see such a personal view of Egypt but to share the experience with their families.

Of course, not everyone can take a trip to visit locations or learn concepts emphasized in the curriculum. That's where TrackStar comes in. TrackStar (www.trackstar.4teachers.org) is a free online program that allows the creation of a VFT by collecting and annotating existing web resources for students to follow. For example, numerous websites on Egypt exist. Teachers can create a "track" in which they list the websites they want students to visit in order from first to last, along with annotations about what students should look for (e.g., specific vocabulary terms).

ACTIVITIES FOR FLUENCY DEVELOPMENT

Fluency is the ability to read with speed, accuracy, and proper expression. It's important because of its direct effect on comprehension. Padak and Rasinski (2008) think of fluency as a bridge that connects decoding to comprehension and "consists of automatizing decoding so that readers can pay attention to constructing meaning" (p. 2). Research has shown that a significant number of students struggle with fluency, which in turn affects their comprehension (Pinnell, Pikulski, Wixson, Campbell, Gough, & Beatty, 1995; Rasinski, & Padak, 1998). However, teachers can provide support to improve students' fluency in many ways. Modeled fluent reading and repeated readings through activities such as readers' theater are two of the most effective. The following sections will focus on ways that technology can enrich these activities.

Modeled Fluent Reading

It is important for students to have a model of what fluent reading sounds like; the most significant model is the teacher. As discussed in this chapter, daily read-alouds by the teacher provide an excellent model of fluent reading. Additionally, online ebooks, discussed in Chapter 5, provide an opportunity for guided practice (i.e., to hear fluent reading while following along with the text). Audiobooks are another excellent source for modeled fluent reading.

Some teachers have a listening center in their classroom where a small group of children sit at a table with a CD/tape player and headphones and listen to a story. However, issues around children's ability to use the equipment appropriately and the need for individualization have caused many teachers to change the concept. MP3 players such as iPods are a great alternative and have become staples in many classrooms.

MP3 players offer many more benefits than audiobooks. Teachers can individualize each child's listening experience. For example, a playlist for a specific child might contain audio books at his or her reading level so the child can follow along with the book as he or she listens (see Figure 4.6). The combination of seeing and hearing the words leads developing readers to improved and more expressive recognition of the words in the text. Playlists can also match a child's specific interests or focus on a particular genre. There are many sources for free audiobooks, which can be downloaded from online sources and the local library (e.g., www.booksshouldbe-free.com). In addition, you can reformat the audio books you may already have on tapes or CDs into MP3 files.

Podcasts for children are also a great source of listening material for MP3 players. Find podcasts for kids by visiting the iTunes website (itunes.apple.com/ca/genre/pod-casts-kids-family). There are great podcasts from Barefoot Books, Children's Fun Story Time, Story Nory, Reading Rockets, and Sesame Street, just to name a few. Additionally, podcasts about different content areas (www.scholastic.com/teachers/article/10-podcasts-teachers-and-kids) are available.

Repeated Reading

Repeated reading has been shown to be the most effective practice for developing fluency (Padak & Rasinski, 2008). Just like practicing notes on a musical instrument makes playing music fluent, practice reading makes reading fluent. Repeated readings

Figure 4.6. Individualized Student Playlists on an iPod

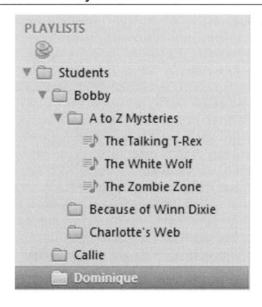

work best when students have an authentic reason for practicing, such as for a performance. Think about how many times an actor rehearses his lines for a play. As he practices, the lines become more automatic and expressive, but the act of repeating the lines never gets dull because he knows this repetition will make him a better performer. This brings us to another important component of performance—an audience. Provide students with an opportunity to perform for a real audience and they will enthusiastically practice, practice, practice!

Choral reading and readers' theater provide two excellent formats for practiced performance. In choral reading, a whole class or group of students read a poem or short piece of text in unison. Several books of poetry written to be read aloud by two voices, such as *Joyful Noise: Poems for Two Voices* by Paul Fleischman (1988), work very well. Give students the opportunity to read the text silently first and then model reading it. Since poetry lends itself to interpretation, students can compare the different ways they think the poem should be read and discuss how the different renditions change the meaning and/or make the reading better. Students can practice reading the text together, or with buddies, multiple times until they are able to perform it as intended.

In Reader's Theater, students have a script and assigned parts, just as in a traditional play, but students read directly from the script rather than memorizing it. Reader's Theater is an interpretive, voice-only performance. Students use their voices to bring the characters to life without sets, props, or costumes. The readers must convey the text in a way so the audience can visualize the story (Martinez, Roser, & Strecker, 1999). This requires a deep understanding of the plot and the characters' motives and actions.

Two important steps of effective implementation of Reader's Theater are selecting the script and providing appropriate support for students. The following guidelines (Reader's Theater, n.d.) will get you started:

1. Begin with very easy scripts at the start, so students don't have to think about how to read the words.
2. Also begin with short scripts; students need to learn to listen to the script just as much as they need to learn to read the script.
3. Select scripts that involve many readers (e.g., scripts that give more readers fewer words).
4. Provide each reader with a separate script, highlighting his or her part.
5. Allow the readers to read the script silently and to read their parts to themselves aloud.

As stated in number two, it is important for students to hear themselves, especially after reading the script a few times. Students can record themselves on MP3 players or other recording devices and play back to assess their performance. Once the students are ready for their final performance, they will need an audience. Invite other classes or parents, or create a podcast using free, easy-to-use computer software such as audacity (www.audacity.com) and GarageBand (www.apple.com/ilife/garageband), or record on an online application such as SoundCloud, discussed in Chapter 2. You may then save the recording as an MP3 file and upload it to an MP3 player, students' blogs, or a classroom website.

With the right script, support, and the opportunity to perform for a real audience, Reader's Theater is very motivating and engaging for students. Children's literature consultant Judy Freeman (as cited in Reader's Theater, n.d.) exclaims:

> If you're searching for a way to get your children reading aloud with comprehension, expression, fluency, and joy, Reader's Theater is a miracle. Hand out a photocopied play script, assign a part to each child, and have the students simply read the script aloud and act it out. That's it. And then magic happens.

CHAPTER 5

Sites and Selection Criteria for Ebooks

After a long period of the dominance of the book as the central medium of communication, the screen has now taken that place.

—Gunter Kress, *Literacy in the New Media Age* (2003, p. 20)

The Internet allows teachers to bring a world of ebooks into the classroom. Some ebooks can only be read online, some can be read online and are also downloadable to e-reader devices or apps, and some are available only as book apps. Some of these ebooks are simply digitized forms of traditional books, whereas others are interactive—students can listen to the book being read, have words pronounced or defined, or engage in conversations about the book. The Internet and many e-reader apps also offer opportunities to learn more about a book's setting, events, and author and to engage in extension activities that enrich the reading experience.

Ebooks offer both opportunities and challenges for teachers and students. Dalton and Proctor (2008) write:

> The dynamic and flexible environment of the Internet offers new opportunities to scaffold and level the playing field so that all individuals are contributing to and benefit from expanded models of literacy . . . reducing the importance of some reader factors, such as word recognition, that have traditionally operated as gatekeepers to literacy, and increasing the importance of other factors, such as self-regulation and multimodal abilities. (p. 299)

This chapter examines the categories and structures of digital books and provides considerations for selecting quality, well-designed ebooks for students as well as ways to maximize students' interactions with ebooks.

ONLINE EBOOKS

This section will discuss ebooks only accessible online. These ebooks fall into two major categories, online read-alouds and interactive storybooks.

Online Read-Alouds

Children enjoy hearing books read aloud by their family, teachers, and librarians who serve as models for reading. One of the major advantages of online books is the capability to integrate audio and video so students can hear and/or view stories being read aloud. This combination supports young children in learning to read by providing models of oral reading. Some ebooks highlight words or phrases as the story is read aloud to promote concepts about print, word recognition, and fluency. Online ebooks range from traditional picturebooks that may be too difficult for younger students to read independently, to "little books" that, if selected according to individual students' reading levels and/or with the support of audio, can be read independently. Let's start with picturebook read-alouds.

Storyline Online (www.storylineonline.net), created by the Screen Actors Guild Foundation, has capitalized on the ability to use streaming video to showcase celebrities such as Elijah Wood, Betty White, Haylie Duff, and James Earl Jones reading and discussing children's picturebooks (see Figure 5.1). Since the story is a video recording, no navigation is required beyond clicking the "Let's Read It!" button. The video shows the celebrity reading as well as the picturebook illustrations (captions of the text are optional). The site includes a summary of each book; information about the author, illustrator, and celebrity reader(s); and related activities. Currently, the site offers 25 picturebooks that would appeal to students in grades K–6. One exceptional example is the reading of *No Mirrors in My Nana's House* written by Ysaye Barnwell (1998) and read by Tia and Tamera Mowry. Included in the video is the song from which the book originated, performed by the acapella quintet Sweet Honey in the Rock, of which the book's author is a member.

A similar online book source is Between the Lions (pbskids.org/lions), which offers several video stories. As the text is read, the words are highlighted so younger students can follow along, tracking text from left to right and top to bottom. Students may

Figure 5.1. Online Read-Aloud from Storyline Online

stop, start, or replay at any point to check their predictions, clarify unknown words, or monitor their understanding.

Most often however, online read-alouds are not video recordings. The vast majority provide a display of the text and illustrations/pictures, as well as an audio recording of the book. The reader must navigate through the story and be able to turn the audio or text on or off as needed. Many texts are read aloud in different languages such as Spanish, French, German, and Japanese (e.g., www.wiredforbooks.org/kids.htm). Texts can be digital versions of classic picturebooks or created specifically for the Internet, thus the quality varies.

In addition to picturebook read-alouds, online ebooks include "little books," written specifically for beginning readers. These books are often written with repetitive text and high frequency words and the text may be highlighted as it is read for support. Several of these books can be found at MightyBook (www.mightybook.com/story_books.html).

Unite for Literacy (www.library.uniteforliteracy.com/us.aspx) offers free access to over 100 simple picture books for read-alouds for preschool, kindergarten, and 1st grade, with new books added each month. The books are written in English and narrated (on demand) in English and in 15 other world and indigenous languages.

Teachers must carefully select online read-alouds to meet individual student's needs. Additionally, for all students to successfully engage with these books, students must understand how they work. The structure or organization of online read-alouds follows that of traditional print; stories are read from start to finish with little or no other functionality. For video recordings of books such as Storyline Online, students need to know how to start, stop, fast forward, and rewind; and turn captions on and off. For books such as Between the Lions (www.pbskids.org/lions), students need to know how to navigate forward and backward in addition to starting and stopping the video. For online books that show the print and pictures accompanied by audio, students will need to learn how to navigate page turns. No matter how simple, it is important for students to become familiar with how to navigate the computer, the Internet, and associated applications and programs. Model and guide students through this process many times to ensure students are actively engaged in a successful read-aloud and do not become frustrated.

Interactive Storybooks

Interactive storybooks transform traditional print stories by adding graphics, sound, animation, and video to create interactive texts, much like a storybook on a CD-ROM. Glasgow (1996) examined the use of CD-ROM storybooks at different stages in children's reading development and found that in the emergent stage they can be helpful in reducing dependence on text by integrating print, images, sound, motion, and color. In addition, students can track text from left to right and top to bottom because the text is highlighted as it is read (see Figure 5.3). Older students can benefit from work with unknown vocabulary since some interactive storybooks have accompanying graphics that show the meaning of the word, which takes into account individual student differences. Further, the interactivity helps students become more personally involved as they learn lessons presented in the storybook.

One outstanding site for interactive storybooks is the TumbleBook Library (www. tumblebooks.com/library/asp/customer_login.asp), a collection of highly popular animated, talking picturebooks for K–5 students, offered through participating public libraries (see Figure 5.2). (More advanced students may turn off the audio and graphics and read the books for themselves.) Some books even include a word helper that defines certain words in the story.

Interactive storybooks have a great deal more functionality than online read-alouds, thus the structure becomes more complicated. Students must understand basic navigation, but potentially, many other functions that may enhance their reading experience. For example, the website for Nick Jr. (www.nickjr.com) has several ebooks featuring the popular television character Dora the Explorer. In Dora's Space Adventure (www.nickjr.com/kids-games/doras-space-adventure.html), the text is shown and read aloud for the first two pages. Then, the story becomes interactive in that the reader is encouraged to count the space creatures Dora encounters. On the first page in which the reader encounters the space creatures, the creatures move and make noise as the cursor moves over them. This may add fun for a young reader, but it also may be distracting and take away from the meaning of the story. On the next page, Dora prompts the reader to click on the creatures to count them. As the cursor moves over each creature, Dora counts in Spanish, providing a unique opportunity to listen to Spanish and learn how to count in Spanish.

Preview interactive storybooks to determine if the interactive features will produce a positive learning experience or distract the reader from comprehension. Additionally, be sure to model the navigation of the interactive features and how to make smart decisions about whether to use features that may be distracting and do not contribute to comprehension of the story.

Figure 5.2. Page from the Interactive Storybook *The Diary of a Worm* (Cronin, 2003)

E-Narratives

Thousands of digitized versions of traditional print books are available for free on the Internet. These books contain no added audio, video, or similar interactive features; however, some include hyperlinks to support navigation to another related part of the text, such as a glossary or a map. A unique and invaluable collection is the International Children's Digital Library (en.childrenslibrary.org). This collection currently includes approximately 4,600 books in 61 languages for children ages 3–13. The browser interface, which is available in 20 languages, allows students to search for new books and retrieve previously read books from categories they can easily understand such as true or make believe, book color or length, places, or how a book makes them feel. An advanced search interface is also available for older students and adults. The collection is focused on books that help students to understand the world around them and the global society in which they live. The books represent exemplary artistic, historic, and literary qualities. (For details on selection criteria, see en.childrenslibrary.org/about/collection.shtml.) Many books are written in dual languages, which is especially beneficial for ELLs, since books in their first language may be difficult to find in print. For instance, the collection currently contains 476 books from Iran written in Farsi (see Figure 5.3 for an example) and 25 books from the Philippines written in Tagalog. The ICDL also has an app that allows users to download books to an iPad or iPhone and a Storykit app that allows students to create their own ebook.

Project Gutenberg (www.gutenberg.org) offers over 42,000 free ebooks, which are traditional print books in the public domain (no longer protected by copyright) that have been digitized. They can be read online or downloaded to e-reader devices. The Rosetta Project (www.childrensbooksonline.org/library.htm) is another digital library that houses digitized versions of classic traditional print books. Examples of these books include *Gulliver's Travels* (Swift, 1892), *Alice's Adventures in Wonderland* (Carroll, 1865), and *The Tale of Peter Rabbit* (Potter, 1902).

Since the structure of e-narratives is similar to traditional print texts, the only functionality students need to become familiar with is the navigation controls. The book may be broken into parts and accessed from an entry point, often a hyperlinked table of contents, so when finished with one chapter, students need to navigate to the table of contents to access the next chapter. The most challenging part of e-narratives may be using the search interface that allows readers to find, select, and read books. However, the exciting aspect of digital libraries such as the International Children's Digital Library and Rosetta Project is that students can choose the books they want to read. As with any independent reading context, students must know how to determine if a book is just right or too hard. Therefore, modeling and guiding students in learning how to use the search interface is essential.

Hybrid Books

A recent trend in children's publishing is hybrid or multi-platform books. These are books that have online components which are integral to the reading experience. The online components go hand-in-hand with the traditional print text; children have

Figure 5.3. Page from the Persian E-Narrative *How Did the Moon Gain Her Spot?* (Taghdis, 1383)

جلو پنجره یک درخت گیلاس بود، پراز شکوفه‌های صورتی.
ماه یک‌بار دیگر لابه‌لای شکوفه‌ها چرخید. دلش نمی‌آمد برود.
شکوفه‌ها بوی لطیفی داشتند، ولی او باید می‌رفت. آخرسر راه افتاد.

Source: Material available at www.childrenslibrary.org.

to read the book to be able to understand the online content, and vice versa. Some include QR barcodes that reveal maps or videos, others have websites with interactive games and videos that are integral to the reading experience.

For example, *The Amanda Project* (Valentino & Kantor, 2009) features three teens who investigate the disappearance of a mutual friend. On a companion website, readers can upload their own "clues" to Amanda's presence. *Skeleton Creek* (Carmon, 2009) alternates between the written diary of Ryan, a housebound teen trying to investigate strange occurrences in his home town, and the video missives of his best friend, Sarah which are accessed by logging onto a website. Another very popular example is The 39 Clues series launched in 2008 by Scholastic beginning with *The Maze of Bones* by Rick Riordan. The series follows Amy Cahill and her brother Dan as they travel the world to hunt for the clues that unlock the family's power. Each book comes with six game cards and an online component that reveals important information about the Cahills and unlocks clues. Ten of the 39 clues can be found within each of the books, but the rest must be found by using the cards and by taking part in online missions. There are currently more than 15 million copies in print worldwide for The 39 Clues series and more than 2 million registered users for the online game and more hybrid book series by Scholastic have been released (e.g., *Infinity Ring, Spirit Animals*).

Ellie Berger, president of Scholastic Trade, describes hybrid books as "21st century storytelling at its best" (Digital Book World, 2013) and in many ways, these books are indicative of the type of online reading/viewing/listening students will need to do to live and work in the 21st century. As previously discussed, to successfully comprehend hybid texts, students must know how to integrate multiple sources of information. Teachers can assist students by teaching the skills and strategies they need to successfully read and comprehend across multiple media (discussed in Chapter 6).

SELECTING ONLINE EBOOKS

Careful selection of digital texts is equally important as the selection of print texts, with a few added considerations. Dalton and Proctor (2008) write:

> Authorship and authority are more elusive, as the democratic space of the Web encourages unvetted publication, bypassing the review and editing processes of established publishing venues, and texts and sites are formed and reformed across multiple authors/designers and over time. Purpose is also less obvious, as websites often have multiple goals, layered and overlapping, overt and covert, in ways not typical of print. (p. 298)

Previewing digital texts is critical to ensure they are appropriate, reader friendly, accessible and contain worthwhile information. When selecting digital texts, teachers must take into account a number of considerations to ensure that it is a quality ebook designed to support the navigational skills of students. The questions in Figure 5.4 will guide your selection.

All these considerations are important individually and in tandem. For example, the digital texts available from Big Universe (www.biguniverse.com) meet many of the criteria outlined in Figure 5.4 but also have features that need to be carefully considered. Some books are free and others available via a paid membership. The digitized versions of traditional print books include books by publishing companies and books created by members (links to publisher and creator information are provided to check credibility). The search interface is easy to use, and the books load quickly into a full screen view. The navigation buttons at the bottom of the page are easy to use, but there is also a link to the publisher's website and another link for purchasing the book. The book works well with ease of access options and is available in eight languages. The site provides the option to search for digital texts by grade level, text level, subject, or category.

After careful review, teachers may determine that many books on the Big Universe site would be excellent when selected purposefully for and by individual students. However, keep in mind that you still need to show the students how to navigate through the site and text, and how to make smart decisions about clicking links that may navigate them away from the book.

EBOOKS ON E-READER DEVICES AND APPS

This section will discuss ebooks that can be electronically downloaded on a digital reading device (e-reader) such as Amazon's Kindle, Barnes and Noble's Nook, and Sony's PRS, or via an e-reader app that can be downloaded on devices such as smart phones, iPods, iPads and other tablet devices.

Figure 5.4. Criteria for Selecting Digital Texts

Quality

- If the text is narrative, does it follow standards for literary merit as evaluated by the different literary elements, including style, setting, character, plot, and theme?
- If the text is informational, is the information accurate and organized in an accessible way that is interesting to the intended audience?
- If the text is poetry, are the readability, subject matter, and form accessible for the intended audience?
- Does the text include information that is culturally or factually inaccurate or misleading?
- Is the text devoid of nostalgia, sentimentality, sarcasm, and didacticism?
- Will the text appeal to readers?
- If there are illustrations, do they support or extend the text in a meaningful way?
- If there are photographs, do they look real?
- If there is audio, does it sound natural and is the text read with appropriate tone, inflection, voice variation, and pacing?
- If there are hyperlinks or other interactive features, do they support or extend the text, or do they have the potential to distract the reader?

Credibility

- Was the site/digital text developed by a reputable company (.com or .net), education institution (.edu), or organization (.org)?
- If the text was developed by an individual, is the author's name and email address available?
- Is there a date that tells you when the digital text was made?
- Does the text include advertising?

Accessibility/Usability

- Does the page take a long time to load?
- If you go to another page, is there a way to return to the first page?
- If the site uses a search engine, is it easy to use and understand?
- If the book or site includes advertising, is it distracting or inappropriate?

Readability

- Does the text indicate a grade or reading level?
- Are the words and images big enough to see?
- Does the text work well with ease of access options such as text magnifier and narration?
- Is the text available in other languages?

E-Reader Devices

In January 2011, Amazon—the creator of the Kindle e-reader—announced that ebooks outsold paperbacks for the first time in the company's history, stating, "For every 100 paperback books Amazon has sold, the Company has sold 115 Kindle books. Additionally, during this same time period the Company has sold three times as many Kindle books as hardcover books" (Amazon.com, 2011). This represents a significant shift in how people are choosing to access and read books. Furthermore, the Scholastic Kids and Family Reading Report (Scholastic, 2013) found that kids who read ebooks are reading more, especially boys, and half of children age 9–17 indicated they would read more books for fun if they had greater access to ebooks.

Depending on the amount of memory, or storage space, e-readers can store between 350 and 1,500 ebooks, newspapers, and magazines from more than 200,000 titles. Some enhanced ebooks contain embedded video, audio, and hyperlinks, and support readers' background knowledge and comprehension. However, most consist only of text.

Although e-reader devices are still not common in classrooms, declining cost, ease of use, and instantly accessible texts will make these devices more proliferate. Ebooks are significantly cheaper than their paperback and hardback counterparts. For example, the 2013 Newbery winner, *The One and Only Ivan* (Applegate, 2012), is approximately $9.00 for the hardback print version on Amazon but is only $4.00 for the Kindle version. In addition, more than a million out-of-copyright books are available completely free of charge via Google Books (see: books.google.com/intl/en/googlebooks/about).

Many ebook devices include interactive tools that allow readers to search for keywords, look up unknown words, change the font size, and listen to the book being read aloud. E-reader devices also allow readers to engage in reading response as they highlight or underline text, insert notes, attach files, or record comments. Larson (2009) found that many of these interactive features can assist teachers with differentiating reading instruction and provide students with individual support. For example, research has found that when e-readers are set up to display only a few words per line, some people with dyslexia can read more easily, quickly, and with greater comprehension (Schneps, Thomson, Chen, Sonnert, & Pomplun, 2013). Additionally, a recent survey on children's attitudes toward reading revealed that struggling readers believe that ebooks are better than print books because they are personal and private and they can still look "cool" when reading, even if the book is at a lower reading level than their classmates' (Scholastic, 2013). However, keep in mind that these interactive features and the excitement for them do not outweigh the quality of the books and how these interactive features align with the personal preferences of the reader (Jones & Brown, 2011).

E-Reader Apps

Many e-reader devices such as the Kindle and Nook also provide free apps that allow the user to download an ebook to a smart phone or tablet device such as the iPad, with the same functions as those on the e-reader device. There are also many other free e-reader apps that offer similar and expanded functions that provide opportunities for significant student interaction and engagement.

Most e-reader apps allow the user to access:

- a purchased ebook
- a free book from Project Gutenberg and other sites
- PDF (portable document format) documents
- online articles
- free digital ebooks from the public library

Additionally, apps such as Subtext (www.subtext.com) allow a teacher to embed instruction and scaffolding right in the pages of the book or document with prompts, videos, information, web links, assignments, and quizzes. Students can annotate text as they read and also discuss the text with classmates. The teacher can set up discussion groups and students can see each other's notes and comments and include web links or video in their notes and comments. Subtext is designed specifically for the K–12 classroom; however there are other apps that offer some of the same features, such as Readmill (readmill.com/ipad), Bookshout (bookshout.com), Ponder (www.ponderi.ng) and Marvin (marvinapp.com).

BOOK APPS

Book apps are similar to ebooks in that they are downloaded to a smart phone or tablet device; however they differ in that book apps usually have high quality graphics, multimedia, and are interactive. When thoughtfully designed, the interdependence of graphics, multimedia, and interactivity can create an immersive experience for the reader that enhances the story's meaning.

Criteria for Selecting Book Apps

Many book apps for children are adaptations of traditional picture books. A good book app puts the story first. Bircher (2012) writes, "A successful picture book app fulfills the requirements of a traditional picture book, but with an extra oomph unique to the digital format. Adaptations of print books present faithful representations with all interactive elements enhancing—not undermining—the original narratives" (p. 78). In addition to extending the original text, Bircher points out that a good picture book app meets the following criteria:

- Utilizes the "drama of turning the page": Many book apps replicate the act of turning a physical page in a picture book with the use of a swipe or arrow that triggers an animated page turn. Just as in a traditional picture book, the page turn should change perspective, redirect feelings for attention, create suspense and drama, and confirm or foil predications. Through the use of animation, book apps can also zoom in on aspects of the illustrated page, synchronizing the readers' attention with the narration.

- Allows the user a customizable experience: Users should be able to turn on or off features such as narration, sound effects, music, and automatic page turns. Additionally, some apps allow the users to record their own narration and create their own story. Users should also be able to advance forward or back through the story easily by accessing an unobtrusive map of the story or thumbnail screenshots. Interactive features embedded in the app that trigger actions can become boring once activated one or more times by the user, so users should be able to quickly move on from these features with a quick tap or swipe.

- Employs intuitive, user-friendly navigation: Written or visual directions such as arrows, buttons, or lights indicating how to navigate through the book and activate interactive features are important and should be easy to understand as the user engages with the book app.

- Provides a surprising and joyful experience: Good book apps integrate meaningful interactive features that invite users to participate in constructing the story. For example, in Figure 5.5, *The Three Little Pigs: A 3-D Fairy Tale* by Nosy Crow, the user can blow into the microphone displayed on the screen to help the wolf blow down the pig's house.

- Encourages repeated use: Some apps incorporate different animations on subsequent readings or features that engage the user in co-creating the story or drawing images that make repeated readings new and engaging. For example, *Don't Let the Pigeon Run This App* by Mo Willems lets users create and record their own stories.

Some educators have expressed concern that, unlike interaction with print texts, the prevalent use of book apps does not build knowledge of early literacy skills. Of particular concern is the practice of simply handing a child a smart phone or iPad and allowing him or her to interact with the ebook independently, since many of the features of a book app serve the traditional function of the adult, including reading the book aloud. Can a book app replace the need for adult interaction?

Recent research by the Joan Ganz Cooney Center (2012) sheds some light on this question. Researchers compared parents reading a basic ebook (no interactive features, like a traditional print book) with their child to parents reading an enhanced ebook (with interactive features, like a book app). They found that parent-child interactions around the basic ebook elicited similar literacy-building actions (e.g., labeling, pointing, and verbal elaboration of story features) to traditional print books. However, interactions around the enhanced ebook prompted nonliteracy related actions such as device-focused talk and actions. The findings concluded,

> Parents and teachers should choose print or basic ebooks to read with children if they want to prioritize literacy-building experiences over ones intended "just for fun." Some

Figure 5.5. Page from the Book App *The Three Little Pigs* (2013)

of the extra features of enhanced ebooks may distract adults and children alike from the story, affecting the nature of conversation and the amount of detail children recall. However, given that appeal is an essential building block for early literacy development, enhanced e-books may be valued for their ability to prompt less motivated young readers toward engagement when they might otherwise avoid text altogether. (5th ¶)

Teachers provide a balanced approach when they conduct read-alouds and shared reading with print texts, and model and demonstrate reading and interacting with an enhanced book or book app with students first, before allowing them to interact with it independently.

There are also chapter book apps and informational book apps (see Figure 5.6) for older readers that may have fewer interactive features but generally should follow the same guidelines for selection. There are several online review sources for book apps that may help teachers with selecting book apps, including the following:

- The American Association of School Librarians (www.ala.org/aasl/standards-guidelines/best-apps)
- The Horn Book Magazine's Best App of the Week (www.hbook.com/category/choosing-books/app-review-of-the-week)
- Kirkus Reviews (www.kirkusreviews.com/book-reviews/ipad)

Figure 5.6. Page from the Book App *March of the Dinosaurs* (2011)

- Publishers Weekly (www.publishersweekly.com/pw/by-topic/childrens/childrens-book-news/index.html)
- Common Sense Media (www.commonsensemedia.org/mobile-app-lists/best-book-apps-kids)

Recommended and Free Book Apps

The following are a few recommended picture book apps for younger readers:

- *A Present for Milo* by Mike Austin (Ruckus Media Group, $5.99)
- *Boats* by Byron Barton (Ocean House Media, $1.99)
- *Big Nate: Comix by U!* by Lincoln Peirce (HarperCollins/Night & Day Studios, $2.99)
- *Don't Let the Pigeon Run This App* by Mo Willems and You (Disney Enterprises, $5.99)
- *The Monster at the End of This Book* by Jon Stone (Callaway Digital Arts, $4.99)
- *The Three Little Pigs: A 3-D Fairy Tale* (Nosy Crow, $5.99)
- *The Waterhole* by Graeme Base (Graeme Base, $2.99)
- *Bats! Furry Fliers of the Night* (Bookerella and Story Worldwide, $2.99)

The following are a few recommended book apps for older readers:

- Creatures of Light: Nature's Bioluminescence (American Museum of Natural History, Free)
- *The Waking Prince* (The Story Elves, $3.99)
- March of the Dinosaurs (Touch Press, $1.99)
- *Dragon, Robot, Gatorbunny* (Chronicle, $9.99)
- *The Middle School Confidential* (Free Spirit Publishing, $2.99)
- *The Fantastic Flying Books of Mr. Morris Lessmore* (Moonbot Studios, $12.99)
- *Building Titanic* (National Geographic, Free)
- *All Around the World* (Barefoot Books, $ 7.99)

The following are a few recommended free book apps:

- *I Love Mountains* (www.forestgiant.com)
- NASA (www.nasa.gov/connect/apps.html)
- The American Museum of Natural History (www.amnh.org/apps)
- National Geographic (www.nationalgeographic.com/apps)
- The Poetry Foundation (www.poetryfoundation.org/mobile)
- DC Comics (www.dccomics.com/tags/dc-comics-app) and Marvel Comics (www.marvel.com/mobile)
- *Aseop's Fables* (www.read.gov/aesop/index.htm)
- iStorybooks (www.istorybooks.co)
- Most libraries also loan ebooks and book apps.

DIGITAL MAGAZINES

In a recent survey of 21,000 children aged 8–16, 57% indicated that they like to read magazines (Clark, 2012). This shouldn't be surprising since magazines offer students current information on many topics of interest to them, written by experts, with appealing layouts and photography. However, magazine subscriptions are expensive and are difficult to maintain since they are not very sturdy. Fortunately, there are many magazines available online. The following is a list of several online magazines:

- Click (PreK–2, www.clickmagkids.com)
- Kids Discover (1–6, www.kidsdiscover.com/kids)
- NASA Science (K–12, www.spaceplace.nasa.gov)
- National Geographic Kids (K–6, www.kids.nationalgeographic.com/kids)
- Highlights for Kids (K–6, www.highlightskids.com)
- Amazing Kids Magazine (3–12, www.mag.amazing-kids.org)
- Sports Illustrated for Kids (3–12, www.sikids.com)

These online magazines contain quality content, including articles, images, and video; however, it is difficult to know when new content is added, and some sites also contain advertising and other extraneous information. Multiplatform applications such as Flipboard (www.flipboard.com) allow users to subscribe to online magazines and then display the informational content-only advertisements are removed. Users can "flip" through the content to find articles, images or videos of interest, save favorite content and make comments. New content is continually added when available. Users can also create their own magazine from the content they find interesting and want to collect and share with others. In this way, students become curators of the content unique to their own interests and curiosities. Other applications that allow users to subscribe and curate information are Zite (www.zite.com) and Pulse (www.pulse.me).

CHAPTER 6

Using E-Tools to Scaffold Comprehension of E-Literature

As the world told becomes the world shown, the texts of the 21st century will require new skills, strategies, and new pedagogies to support students' transactions with these multimodal, multimedia texts.

—Frank Serafini (2012, p. 27)

Over the last 3 decades, research has supported the potential of technology to support reading achievement and comprehension. The inherent flexibility of digital environments and applications expands opportunities for comprehension and reduces learning barriers. The ebooks discussed in the previous chapter allow students to listen to digital text, thus bypassing decoding or fluency issues, and providing vocabulary and background knowledge support through embedded hyperlinks. This strengthens the teacher's ability to differentiate instruction and better meet the needs of today's increasingly diverse classrooms. Young children learning to read and struggling readers benefit from the support of hearing a story read aloud and from the opportunity to read along to stories written on their reading level. English language learners (ELLs) may especially benefit from listening to stories in their first language and in English, and students learning a language other than English would benefit in the same way. Additionally, these contexts and applications offer students extensive opportunities for guided practice with multiple texts over time.

The Internet provides access to a vast source of information on endless topics that can provide background knowledge for language arts and content-area instruction. Embedded links, images, video, and audio all support students in understanding content and concepts in ways not provided by printed texts.

As much as the digital environment supports comprehension, it also increases the importance of other factors such as self-regulation and multimodal abilities. Therefore, it's important to design instruction that supports digital learning. A logical starting point is to consider print-based comprehension. Coiro (2003) writes:

> [S]ome tasks on the Internet ask readers to extend their use of traditional comprehension skills to new contexts for learning, while others, like electronic searching and telecollaborative inquiry projects, demand fundamentally different sets of new literacies not currently covered in most language arts curriculums. (p. 463)

In other words, reading digital text requires a combination of familiar comprehension processes and skills—such as locating main ideas, summarizing, and inferring—and new processes required to read digital text formats, such as evaluating hyperlink information, and the credibility and relevance of online information. The purpose of this chapter is to support literacy teachers in preparing to teach with, about, and through digital texts. With this in mind, the chapter discusses how to apply well-validated approaches to teaching comprehension with print materials to the design of the digital environment before, during, and after reading (see Table 6.1).

BEFORE READING: DIRECT INSTRUCTION AND MODELING

As with traditional print texts, teachers need to provide direct instruction and teacher modeling on the reading process as it relates to students' ability to apply strategic behaviors for comprehending digital text. Coiro (2003) argues that this is even more important when working with digital texts; that is, "Modeling how to use strategies flexibly to solve different comprehension tasks becomes even more important as technologies rapidly change and new forms of literacy emerge" (p. 463).

An effective modeling strategy used with print-based reading to assess students' use of comprehension strategies is the think-aloud. Thinking aloud while reading aloud makes the invisible processes of reading visible and allows "all students to hear how others sleuth out and make sense of all these text clues so that they can recognize and adopt these strategies as their own" (Wilhelm, 2001, p. 19). After observing the teacher model the think-aloud process, students can use think-alouds to vocalize the strategies they are using and to help students become aware of their strategy use.

Kymes's (2005) research on print-based think-alouds and online comprehension found that many strategies used by good readers are also important to comprehension of online information. These strategies include:

- awareness of purpose
- skimming, scanning, and reading selectively
- activating prior knowledge and maintaining the dialectic
- discovering new meanings of words
- rereading and note-taking for retention of key information
- interpreting or paraphrasing text and "conversing" with the author
- evaluating text structure and quality
- reviewing information

Kymes (2005) contends that teachers can use think-alouds as an instructional tool to model appropriate comprehension strategies when using multimedia and ICTs. Teachers can project a website on a screen so all students can observe how they navigate while listening to them think-aloud about strategy use. For example, the teacher might read a website passage and model how to figure out an unknown word. The teacher

Table 6.1. Considerations for Comprehension Instruction in Digital Environments

	Student considerations	Teacher preparation and instructional support
Before reading	• Individual students' needs • Students' background knowledge of content • Students' knowledge of digital environments • Students' knowledge of strategies for comprehension within digital environments	• Select quality digital texts • Provide a clear purpose for reading • Build background knowledge • Provide direct instruction and modeling of how to maneuver within digital environments • Provide direct instruction and modeling of how to use strategies for effective comprehension with digital text
During reading	• Students' ability to monitor their reading comprehension	• Provide opportunities to use multiple supports within digital texts such as accessing vocabulary definitions and additional background information, annotating and highlighting main ideas and critical information
After reading	• Students' need for further connections with the text that extend and deepen understanding	• Provide opportunities for students to extend and deepen their understanding of text through activities that require students to communicate, collaborate, and create

might say, "I don't know this word, but since it is red, I know it is a link. If I click on the word, it might provide the definition or take me to another site that gives more context. But I want to be careful not to click too many links that lead me away from this site." Teachers should encourage students to engage in this same self-dialogue to become aware of their own comprehension strategies when navigating online environments. As Kymes (2005) states:

> For students to develop higher levels of understanding, explicit or direct instruction in metacognitive strategies that regulate self-awareness, self-control, and self-monitoring are necessary. Only with specific instruction will students be able to use the technologies, such as online information sources, effectively and productively. (p. 498)

The IRT lessons for this chapter demonstrate strategic comprehension strategies for reading digital texts.

IRT LESSON FOR YOUNGER STUDENTS: COMPREHENSION STRATEGIES FOR READING DIGITAL TEXTS

Phase 1: Teacher modeling

Step 1: Planning the lesson. You may be concerned that the interactive features of digital texts will distract students rather than engage them in deep reading. One way to scaffold students' effective engagement with interactive storybooks is to read aloud and model the use of the storybook online. By modeling and thinking aloud about how to strategically use the interactive features of digital texts, teachers show students how to interact and problem solve to enhance and extend understanding.

Step 2: Introduce the lesson. Tell the students that readers of traditional and digital texts use photos and illustrations to understand concepts within the text (point out such a feature in a traditional nonfiction or fiction book). Explain how this text aid helps readers see the details in something and provides them with extra visual information to comprehend at a deeper level. Then make the same connection to digital text. Explain that digital texts often have photos and illustrations as well as interactive features that expand or extend the photos and illustrations to provide even more information.

Step 3: Model the process. Using a projected image of a digital text (or by seating the students closely around a monitor), use the think-aloud strategy to model how a particular interactive illustration in a digital text helps you to see the details in something or understand what you have read at a deeper level. *The Runaway Rabbit*, featuring Clifford the Big Red Dog, is a good example to illustrate this (pbskids.org/clifford/stories/rabbit.html). This e-story includes an audio read-aloud and interactive illustrations. When the red text is clicked, the illustrations change (see Figure 6.1).

To model the strategy, begin by displaying the first page and reading the directions. Then show how you follow the directions: click on the first line of text, listen to the story on the page, and then look at the illustration.

Think aloud about how the illustration of Clifford shows what is going on in the text and helps you visualize the story.

Then click on the second line of text, listen to the story, and acknowledge that the illustration has changed. Think aloud about how this differs from traditional print texts and how the new illustration adds to your understanding of the story.

This may also be a good time to discuss what to do if you didn't understand why the illustration changed or didn't hear the audio. Good readers—no matter what medium they are reading—stop and reread when there is something they don't understand. Model clicking the first or second line of text again and fixing up what you didn't understand. Navigate to the next page and run through the think-aloud strategy again.

Phase 2: Teacher and student demonstrations

If your students have access to desktop computers or laptops, have them work in pairs to access the site (which could be bookmarked on the computers), and navigate

Figure 6.1. Interactive Illustrations from *The Runaway Rabbit*

Source: www.pbskids.org/clifford/stories/rabbit.html

to the next page in the e-story. If students do not have access to computers, project or show the next page from your computer.

Ask students to follow the directions you just modeled. This time, however, have them think aloud with a partner about how the first illustration informed their understanding of the story and how the new illustration extended their understanding of the story. Remind students that they should stop and reread if there is something they don't understand.

Allow one or two partners to share their thinking with the whole class. Then create an anchor chart with strategic behaviors for understanding digital text discussed in the lesson (anchor charts highlight specific guidelines or behaviors for performing a particular strategy and are discussed further in Chapter 7).

Bring the lesson to a close by engaging the students in a discussion about the importance of using interactive illustrations to assist with comprehension when reading digital text.

Phase 3: Independent practice

Give students the opportunity to engage with the online storybook independently during centers (such as listening center or reading center) or during independent reading time.

IRT LESSON FOR OLDER STUDENTS: COMPREHENSION STRATEGIES FOR READING DIGITAL TEXTS

Phase 1: Teacher modeling

Step 1: Planning the lesson. Often, ebooks for older readers fall into the category of e-narratives, which do not have the same interactive features to support readers such as audio, highlighted text, or pop-up definitions. However, reading e-narratives on a computer or e-reader device or app allows the reader instant access to word definitions or to search for information. On most computers and tablet devices, highlighting and clicking on a word provides the user with the option of getting the definition or conducting a search for the word. However, identifying unknown words, hard-to-pronounce words, or unfamiliar topics when reading is a strategic process that students must use to understand text. In a digital environment, students not only need to identify unknown words and topics, but need to infer whether accessing the definition or searching the topic will support understanding or lead to unnecessary or off-topic information. By modeling and thinking aloud about how to strategically access word definitions or topic searches to enhance and extend understanding, you can help students see how to infer and problem solve.

Step 2: Introduce the lesson. Remind the students that when they encounter words they don't know how to pronounce or words they don't understand in traditional text, they use context clues and word parts to problem solve (model this process with a print text). Explain that unlike traditional texts, digital texts allow the reader to access the definition or search for information on a topic. Caution students that accessing this information may not always be helpful. Reiterate that good readers think carefully before deciding to define or search for a word.

Step 3: Model the process. Use the think-aloud strategy to model how to identify unknown words and how to decide whether to click a word within the text. *Gulliver's Travels* by Jonathan Swift (1892) is an e-narrative for older readers (the e-narrative can be accessed via the Project Gutenberg site: www.gutenberg.org/ebooks/829) that will be used as an example in this lesson.

Begin by reading the text: "My father had a small estate in Nottinghamshire; I was the third of five sons. He sent me to Emmanuel College in Cambridge at fourteen years old, where I resided three years, and applied myself close to my studies . . ." (Swift, 1892). Then model how to identify unknown words and how to decide whether to define a word or search a topic. Explain to students that even though you don't know exactly where Nottinghamshire is in London, you are not going to search for it because you don't think additional information about this place will give you a better understanding of the story at this point in your reading. This is because, as you read on, you see that the main character was sent to Cambridge when he was 14; therefore, it is more likely that the story will take place in Cambridge than in Nottinghamshire, so more information about the school he attended in Cambridge might be helpful in understanding the story.

Next, model highlighting and clicking the words *Emmanuel College* and selecting the option to search, which opens a new window with the search results. More than likely, one of the first search results will be the college's website. Open the website and read some of the information about Emmanuel College (e.g., founded 1584, University of Cambridge; closely associated with the Puritan movement). Explain that since you didn't have background knowledge about Emmanuel College, this information was helpful because you now know the university's age and religious affiliation. Also note that this information lets you know the environment in which the main character will be living, which may be important to the character's actions. There is also a picture of the college, which might help you visualize the story's setting. Model navigating back to the story and reading on.

Phase 2: Teacher and student demonstrations

If your students have access to desktop computers or laptops, have them work in pairs to access the site and navigate to the same page in the e-narrative. If students do not have access to computers, have them complete the guided practice from the projection or from your computer screen.

Ask students to continue reading the text. Request that they think aloud with a partner about whether defining a word or searching a topic will clarify or extend their understanding of the story.

Allow one or two partners to share their thinking with the class. Then create an anchor chart with strategic behaviors of understanding digital text.

Phase 3: Independent practice

Give students the opportunity to engage with e-narratives individually during independent reading time.

Follow-up activities:

Present other minilessons to students to advance and deepen their knowledge of strategies for effectively reading digital text. See Figure 6.2 for suggested minilessons on the skills and strategies for effective reading on the Internet.

Figure 6.2. Minilessons for Teaching the Skills and Strategies to Effectively Reading on the Internet

Navigation skills

- Selecting search strategies that best accomplish a particular task
- Maintaining focus on a task rather than becoming distracted by interesting but irrelevant information
- Navigating within a text for a particular purpose

Comprehension strategies

- Selecting and using multiple multimodal features of digital text, such as interactive illustrations and embedded video or links to problem solve, clarify, extend understanding
- Using links within text to make connections to background knowledge

Strategic behaviors

- Using knowledge of text structure and genre to predict and anticipate digital text features that may be useful
- Asking questions before, during, and after reading, and recognizing that Internet resources are often helpful to better understand a problem
- Previewing or surveying a text before reading to activate background knowledge and determine the text's organization
- Rereading when meaning breaks down
- Using text aids such as linked words or pictures to illuminate and extend meaning
- Marking texts and recording notes (refer to the following section)

Comprehension skills

- Using inferential skills such as inferring contents behind a hyperlink and knowing when Internet content is likely to be useful
- Using literal skills such as using a site map to determine sequence of events or story details
- Using critical skills such as using knowledge of URL endings to determine what purposes might be served by information at a site or to assist with determining if the information may be fact or opinion; identifying the author's viewpoint or stance; critiquing the quality of information; and making a judgment about the value of the information based on the purposes for reading

DURING READING: MONITORING COMPREHENSION

Good readers constantly monitor their understanding of what they read; if they didn't, there would be no benefit to reading. The effective reader must self-regulate, monitor comprehension, and take action to resolve confusions by initiating fix-up strategies. When good readers read, they exhibit behaviors that indicate the strategies they use for solving problems and sustaining meaning. For example, the reader might jot a note in the margin of the text, flag a particular passage with a sticky note, or mark an unknown word. Such behaviors represent critical moments in literacy learning, as they indicate the reader's attempt to monitor comprehension.

The digital text environment can also support self-regulation and monitoring of comprehension. In some ways, a digital environment can extend monitoring and self-regulation strategies in ways that traditional print environments cannot. Two very important scaffolds for supporting monitoring and self-regulation—online annotations and vocabulary and background knowledge—are discussed in the following sections.

Online Annotations

Sticky notes have become a popular tool to assist students with monitoring comprehension, as students use them to write thoughts, questions, or unknown words while reading independently. WebNotes (www.webnotes.net) is an online tool that is the digital equivalent of sticky notes.

When WebNotes is downloaded to a computer, a toolbar appears below the address bar of the Internet browser. WebNotes allows the user to create sticky notes within any web environment. Figure 6.3 shows a portion of Chapter 1 from *Call of the Wild* (London, 1903) with sticky notes created by a reader. The reader has also highlighted part of the opening sentence, another feature of WebNotes, and created a sticky note to indicate why.

At this point, you might be thinking that WebNotes performs in the same way as sticky notes and highlighters in a print environment. However, a unique aspect of WebNotes is that it not only saves the notes for the reader but organizes the notes in a folder and provides a link to the site (see Figure 6.3). Students may create a new folder for every digital book or website in which they use sticky notes or where highlighting is used. Another feature allows the reader to share his or her notes with others via email or Twitter—a great feature for students who are participating in a book club or conducting a research assignment.

WebNotes is extremely easy to use. Just click on the sticky note icon and a virtual note pops up on the webpage. The note can be dragged to any place on the page. Young students could easily use this feature, though typing the note may require more effort and time than for older students with more advanced typing skills. One click on the highlighter icon and the cursor turns into a virtual highlighter that readers can drag across the text to highlight it.

WebNotes (or other sticky note programs available such as Diigo) provides a record of students' comprehension strategy use. These notes are invaluable for not only assessing individual student's comprehension processes in digital environments, but for keeping track of all students over time to inform future teaching decisions.

Vocabulary and Background Knowledge

As discussed in Chapter 4, vocabulary knowledge is critical for students' comprehension of text. Word knowledge is multifaceted, meaning that it is developed over time and different contexts. Each student possesses differentiated knowledge of individual words that ranges from no knowledge to rich, decontextualized knowledge of a word's meaning. Comprehension of a word is easier if the reader has some background

Figure 6.3. WebNotes, Sticky Notes, and Highlighting of Chapter 1 from *Call of the Wild* (London, 1903)

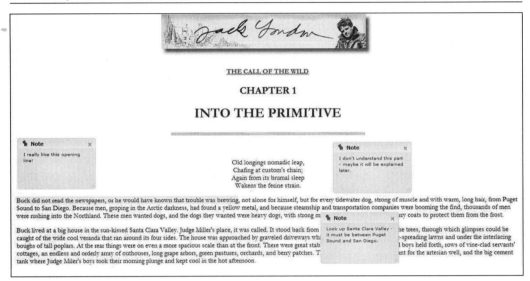

Source: london.sonoma.edu/Writings/CallOfTheWild/chapter1.html

knowledge of the word concept; conversely, comprehension may be harder to attain if the concept is new or difficult. It is essential to provide students with interesting, rich, and robust vocabulary instruction that will inspire interest and awareness of words. However, when reading independently, students must monitor their own knowledge of words and initiate strategies for figuring out unknown words. Beck, Perfetti, and McKeown (1982) state:

> Students need to notice words in their environments whose meaning they do not know. They need to become aware of and explore relationships among words in order to refine and fully develop word meanings. Indeed, being curious about the meaning of an unknown word that one enounters and about how it relates to other words is a hallmark of those who develop large vocabularies. (p. 13)

The digital environment can offer vocabulary support—for example, an online dictionary—for exploring word and concept knowledge. In the e-narrative of the *Tale of Peter Rabbit* (Potter, 1902), Mrs. Rabbit goes to town to buy five currant buns. It is likely that a young reader will not know the word and is curious as to what a currant bun is. When the student highlights the word and then clicks the mouse, a dialog box opens that allows her to display the definition of the word (this is slightly different depending on the platform and browser). Some browsers provide the option to listen to the pronunciation of the word, and to double-click on any unknown word within the definition to see the definition of that word and listen to its pronunciation.

Additionally, online dictionaries and thesauri are also good resources for students that offer additional supports and can be added to any computer as a toolbar, plug-in or widget. For example, on www.dictionary.com, if the student types a word into the search box and clicks the Spanish icon, the definition will be presented in Spanish. Merriam-Webster's ESL Learner's dictionary (www.learnersdictionary.com) presents the definition in very simple, easy-to-understand terms. Similarly, Kid's Word Central (www.wordcentral.com) offers a student dictionary with very simple, easy to understand definitions. The visual dictionary (visual.merriam-webster.com and www.snappywords.com) presents a picture of the word, which in the case of *currant* is very helpful.

When students have accessed the appropriate source for the best definition, they can return to the story and continue reading. However, it would be simple for students to open a sticky note and write the word they looked up, along with their understanding of the word as it is used in the story. This provides the teacher with information on the strategies students are using when they encounter unknown words, so the teacher can provide additional opportunities to learn about the word in different contexts.

The student could also choose the option to conduct a search and the browser will open to a page displaying the search results for the word *currant*. This option might be useful if students are conducting research and need multiple sources of information, or are checking one source against another. However, it is easy to see how this option could distract students from reading; therefore, be sure to teach them effective search strategies before enabling this function.

AFTER READING: DEEPENING TEXT CONNECTIONS AND RESPONSES

Literature extension activities allow students authentic ways to respond to reading. The Internet provides abundant choices for students to respond to literature with plays, re-tellings, poems, or stories. Plus, the Internet makes it easy to share these responses with parents, grandparents, and other relatives, as well as children from around the world.

Virtual Author Visits

There is something magical about meeting authors, listening to them as they describe what inspires them and as they read their works. However, these visits can be very expensive and time-consuming for schools. Although there is no substitute for in-person author visits, virtual author visits are an affordable alternative that offers access to authors who are geographically distant or prefer not to travel. A quick Internet search will produce authors' websites, email addresses, and their publishers' contact information.

Virtual author visits can be conducted via email, blog or bulletin board site, virtual chat, or live broadcast via software such as Skype or Google Hangout. The type of communication technology, the cost, and date/time frame for the visit will be a decision made between the author and publisher, and the teacher. It can take some time to work out the details, so take this into consideration in the overall time frame of the event. Figure 6.4 offers some suggestions for preparing for the visit; this should help to ensure that it goes smoothly and is meaningful for all involved.

Another way to bring authors into the classroom is through online author videos (also called webcasts). Reading Rockets (www.readingrockets.org) is an educational

Figure 6.4. Preparing for a Virtual Author Visit

- Be sure you have access to multiple copies of the author's works.
- Read and discuss the author's works well in advance of the visit. Depending on the number and type of books, this may take at least 3 to 4 weeks.
- Collect students' questions for the author ahead of time.
- Discuss "netiquette" and discussion procedures with the students.
- Check and double check that equipment and software are working, and design a backup plan in case of technical difficulties.
- Use a projector to broadcast the computer screen or webcam so all students can see the communication.
- If connecting via email, blog, bulletin board, or virtual chat, be sure students read all posts before asking follow-up questions.
- Monitor the time and allow students to ask impromptu questions if time permits.

initiative of the public broadcasting station WETA in Washington, DC. In addition to information and resources on how young kids learn to read, the site hosts over 100 videos of renowned children's authors and illustrators such as Chris Raschka, Eric Carle, Walter Dean Myers, and Patricia Polacco. The site also provides a transcript of the interview, a biography of the author/illustrator's life, and a bibliography of the author/illustrator's works. Other videos are available via the National Book Festival, sponsored by the Library of Congress, and held annually since 2001. This festival brings more than 70 award-winning authors, illustrators, and poets to the mall in Washington, DC to talk about their books. Each presentation is videotaped and published online (www.loc.gov/bookfest). The site now features videos of over 200 children's and young adult authors and illustrators.

Almost all authors have a website or are included in their publisher's website. Author websites often offer a showcase of the author's works, appearances, interviews, and speeches, as well as other news about the author. In addition, some authors maintain a blog that updates readers on their daily lives, their writing, or their opinions on various topics.

Teachers and librarians can use these websites and blogs to assist students in getting to know the author, resulting in a deeper understanding of the author's works.

One 1st-grade class conducted an author study on Mem Fox. After reading a few of Fox's books aloud to the students, the teacher, Mrs. Altland, shared Mem Fox's website with them (www.memfox.net/welcome.html). Since she didn't have a projector, she gathered the students around the computer in a shared reading fashion and read aloud some information about Mem Fox. As she did so, Mrs. Altland thought aloud about how she decided to click on certain hyperlinks or which buttons to use to navigate back and forth within the website. In this way, she modeled the decisionmaking process necessary to finding information while reading.

After reading about Mem Fox, Mrs. Altland created an anchor chart with the students on which they recorded information learned from the website, along with the books they had read in which they could see a connection to Mem Fox's life (see Figure 6.5). From the author information gained through the website, the students were able to make important connections between Mem Fox's life and stories.

Figure 6.5. Anchor Chart of Information Learned from Mem Fox's Website and Connections to Her Writing

- She was born in Australia (*Possum Magic*).
- She moved to Africa when she was a little girl.
- Here parents were missionaries who lived on a farm (*Hattie and the Fox*).
- Wilfrid Gordon McDonald Partridge was her father's name (*Wilfrid Gordon McDonald Partridge*).
- She went to college in London. She liked the Beatles, wore miniskirts, and liked to dye her hair.
- Mem didn't get to know her grandfather until he was 90 years old and living in a nursing home (*Sophie*).
- When Mem lived on the farm in Africa, her mom worried about the dangers of the African wildlife (*Possum Magic*).
- She was a younger sister (*Koala Lou*; *Harriet, You'll Drive Me Wild!*).
- She has written 53 children's books.
- Her first book was *Possum Magic*.

Google Lit Trips

Wouldn't it be great if the students learning about Mem Fox could visit Australia and experience the places they read about? Well, guess what? Now they can, through Google Lit Trips! Google Lit Trip was created by Jerome Burg, a former English teacher who combined the excitement of a road trip with the interactive technology and satellite imagery of Google Earth to create the innovative experience of a journey similar to those taken by characters in literature.

The Google Lit Trip site (www.googlelittrips.com) has many "ready-made" Lit Trips for teachers and students to use that are categorized by grade level (K–2, 3–5, 6–8, and 9–12). Several Lit Trips have been created by Burg; however, teachers and students are taking his lead and creating their own Lit Trips and sharing them online. Melanie Turner, an instructional technology specialist for Colquitt County Schools in Georgia, created *Possum Magic* by Mem Fox. On this Lit Trip to Australia, students will visit the cities of Adelaide, Melbourne, Sydney, Brisbane, Darwin, Perth, and the state of Tasmania. Teresa Pombo Pereira, a Portuguese language teacher, created the Portuguese-language Google Lit Trip *Os Lusíadas* by Luís Vaz de Camões, and authors Marc Aronson and Marina Budhos participated in the creation of the Google Lit Trip for their book, *Sugar Changed the World* (see Figure 6.6).

If you have never been "lit-trippin," you will need to download the free Google Earth program (www.google.com/earth/index.html) and familiarize yourself with how it works. Then check out a ready-made Lit Trip to get a feel for how the program works in action. When you are comfortable with the program, you might want to create your own Lit Trip. A demonstration video is available at the Google Lit Trips site from the Google Lit Trips main webpage to show you how to use the program. Burg suggests that the best Lit Trips need not involve long journeys but need to revolve around books with a strong sense of place. As you plan a Lit Trip, think about information that will help your students envision places they have never seen. Consider linking to references

Figure 6.6. Screen Shot of *Sugar Changed the World* Google Lit Trip

Sugar Changed the World
by Marc Aronson and Marina Budhos

An Author Collaboration

ATLANTIC SLAVERY
Plantations of Enslaved Africans

SUGAR CHANGED THE WORLD

"When husband-and-wife team Marc Aronson and Marina Budhos realized that both their family histories involved the sugar industry, they took it as a challenge...The story builds on what many young scholars already know and adds many details. For example, slavery in the United States is a typical school lesson, but the authors disclose that the other 96 percent of enslaved Africans worked in the sugar industry in other parts of the world."
- *2010 Best for Teens: Sugar Changed the World, by Marc Aronson & Marina Budhos*

Source: www.googlelittrips.com/GoogleLit/6-8/Entries/2011/2/9_Sugar_Changed_the_World-by_Marc_Aronson_and_Marina_Budhos.html

that will give students a better understanding of the story's historical, cultural, and geographical context.

After students become familiar with Google Lit Trips, engage them in the process of designing their own trips individually or in small groups. The power of students designing their own Lit Trip can provide an even deeper layer of understanding to a text. As students read, they can look for significant locations or information to add to their map. For example, the Expedition Literature Trip *Into the Wild* by Jon Krakauer is just one of several Lit Trips developed by the students of Thomas Cooper of The Walker School in Marietta, Georgia. Students tracked the journey of the book's main character, Chris McCandless, from Emory University through Arizona, California, Oregon, British Columbia, and finally to Alaska, where his journey ended. Each map marker includes information about the location as it relates to the main character, photos, and links to sources the students researched. Students can also add place markers to pose questions that can be used by the teacher and other students for further research or class discussions.

Book Reviews and Book Talks

Online book reviews provide another avenue for students to respond to reading that has an authentic audience. Potentially hundreds, even thousands of people could read the review, which in turn, may influence whether they decide to read the book. These reviews also provide examples of well-written responses to reading. Some online booksellers such as Amazon and Barnes and Noble offer readers the opportunity to post book reviews. Book reviews by children are available at the following nonprofit websites:

- Kids Reads (www.kidsreads.com), which is part of The Book Report Network, houses hundreds of reviews.
- Spaghetti Book Club (www.spaghettibookclub.org) contains "book reviews by kids for kids."
- World of Reading (www.worldreading.org), which is hosted by the Ann Arbor District Library of Michigan, USA, has thousands of searchable reviews.

Book talks are brief teasers shared with others as a way of enticing them to read a particular book. A 4th-grader offered the following book talk about *Love, Ruby Lavender* (Wiles, 2001):

Love, Ruby Lavender is a hilarious book by Deborah Wiles. This book is funny from the very beginning, when 9-year-old Ruby and her grandmother, Miss Eula, steal chickens from Peterson's Egg Ranch. Miss Eula and Ruby write letters back and forth to each other throughout the book, which are very funny. This book is also about standing up for yourself, forgiveness, and friendship. So, don't be a chicken and read this book!

The student who had written the book talk read it to his class and his delivery was amazing! His intonation, pacing, and enthusiasm were contagious and sold many of his classmates on the book. Although posting this book talk on the student's blog or on the class webpage would allow other students to read it, doing so might not persuade potential readers in the same way as a live book talk. Therefore, creating podcasts of students reading their book talks (and posting the podcasts on the student's blog or the class webpage) is an excellent way to engage students in sharing their reading with others and persuading others to read. It also is ideal for practicing fluency (see Chapter 4 for more on podcasting and fluency). The following websites provide written, audio, and video examples of book talks:

- Scholastic: www.teacher.scholastic.com/products/tradebooks/booktalks.htm
- Booktalks: www.booktalker.blogspot.com
- Bookwink: www.bookwink.com
- Science Books & Films Booktalks: beta.sbfonline.com/pages/booktalkshome. aspx
- Brookline Book Review Podcasts: www.runkle.org/Podcasts/index.html
- Arleta Elementary School Podcasts: www.ppsmultimedialibrary.blogspot. com/2007/03/new-booktalks-podcasts.html

Book Trailers: The Book Talk Transformed

Like book talks, book trailers are designed to entice students to read specific books. However, book trailers open up the modes and media students use to communicate. Students use video, images, transition effects, music, voice recordings, and written text to share their thinking, interpretations, and critiques of the books they read. The effect of layering the media can potentially deepen meaning construction beyond what is possible with only a single media such as text or audio. PowerPoint, Animoto, Voice-Thread, iMovie, and Movie Maker are just a few of the many online or computer-based tools students can use to create book trailers. Animoto and Voicethread also have tablet apps, and Pixntell (www.pixntell.com) is an app-based program for creating short image-based book trailers.

Book trailers are essentially commercials for books, similar to movie trailers, with which many students will be familiar. They are cliffhangers, providing just enough information to interest the reader, but not so much that they give away the plot. Movie trailers are notorious for highlighting the action by showing clips of car chases, explosions, and fights, but do little in the way of conveying the essence of the story. A good book trailer does both.

To engage students in creating book trailers, it's essential that you first find examples of good book trailers and share them with students. A good resource for finding book trailers is Book Trailers for Readers (www.booktrailersforreaders.com). Ensure that students can revisit these examples as digital mentor texts.

Good book trailers convey the essence of the story without giving away too much. Diagramming the plot in advance can assist students with selecting important events to include and determining where to leave a cliffhanger. See www.readwritethink.org/files/resources/interactives/plot-diagram for an interactive tool for plot diagramming.

Storyboards are a planning tool to help students *outline* and *organize* a book trailer scene by scene. Viewed in sequence, storyboards become a road map for the book trailer.

Encourage students to use a variety of multimedia to create layers of meaning. The storyboard template in Figure 6.7 allows students to think about the layers of meaning as well as the layout of the book trailer. Conduct IRT lessons that demonstrate and provide guided opportunities for teaching students to understand how visual, auditory, and print come together to create meaning and emotion and how to integrate these sources of information.

Group students together to work on book trailers. Discussion, collaboration, and planning around the story enriches thinking about books. Also be sure to provide opportunities for students to share their book trailers with one another and give feedback. Book trailers can be posted on students' blogs or class webpages to elicit additional feedback.

WebQuests

A WebQuest facilitates the acquisition, integration, and extension of a vast amount of information through tasks specifically designed to engage the learner in analysis and demonstration of understanding. According to Bernie Dodge (San Diego State University) and Tom March (ozline.com), creators of the WebQuest:

Figure 6.7. Storyboard Template for Creating Book Trailers

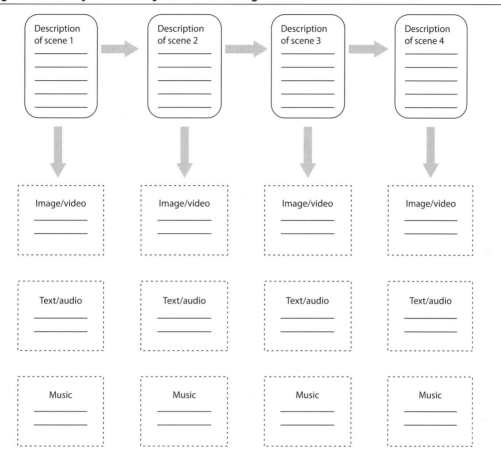

A WebQuest is an inquiry-oriented activity in which most or all of the information used by learners is drawn from the Web. WebQuests are designed to use learners' time well, to focus on using information rather than looking for it, and to support learners' thinking at the levels of analysis, synthesis and evaluation. (edweb.sdsu.edu/webquest/overview.htm, ¶ 2)

Though WebQuests cross the curriculum, literature-based WebQuests center the experience on reading by using books as the focal point for activities. Students might explore the theme, characters, plot, or setting of the book being studied.

WebQuests can be either long term or short term, depending on the instructional goal. Short-term WebQuests can take from one to three sessions and generally involve the learner in knowledge acquisition and integration of new information. Long-term WebQuests can take anywhere from one week to one month, and involves the learner in extending and refining information through analysis and demonstrations.

The design of a WebQuest is critical to its effectiveness as an instructional resource. WebQuests consist of an introduction, task, process, resources, and evaluation. These components create an effective learning environment in which learners become oriented to an interesting, doable task with the resources and guidance to complete the task, including how they will be evaluated.

- **Introduction:** The purpose of the introduction is to draw the reader into the learning situation by relating to the reader's interests, goals, and background knowledge and by providing an engaging description of a compelling question or problem addressed by the WebQuest.
- **Task:** The task focuses learners on what they are going to do—specifically, the culminating performance or product that drives all the learning activities. The task requires synthesis of multiple sources of information, and/or taking a position, and/or going beyond the data given and making a generalization or product.
- **Process:** This section outlines how the learners will accomplish the task. Scaffolding includes clear steps, resources, and tools for organizing information. The process readers should proceed through to complete the project is broken down into clearly described steps. There is variety in the activities performed and/or roles and perspectives to be taken on by the reader.
- **Resources:** The links to web resources are pertinent to the task, make excellent use of the web, and are working. Using the features of WebNotes discussed earlier, students could easily mark and keep track of the information they find from multiple sources for synthesis later.
- **Evaluation:** This section describes the evaluation criteria needed to meet performance and content standards. Explicit tasks describe how students will demonstrate their knowledge. The product reflects this growth (see Chapter 10 for more information on assessment of new literacies).

A WebQuest can provide a structured and scaffolded environment for students to engage more deeply in understanding the story after reading. For ELLs, additional considerations are linguistic features (simple tenses, concise language, no colloquial language), multimedia features (multimodal presentation of information, linked websites present different sources and perspectives and online bilingual dictionary) and organizational features (consistent font and formatting that focuses the reader and chunk information, relevant resources) (Sox & Rubinstein-Ávila, 2009).

Two resources for finding WebQuests based on literature are Literature-based Web-Quests (projects.edtech.sandi.net/projects/literature.html) and Eduscape's WebQuest list (www.eduscapes.com/tap/topic4.htm). As students become familiar with the structure of WebQuests and efficient at searching for information on the Internet, they can create their own WebQuests.

CHAPTER 7

Writing Online

> Writing is a complex, multifaceted, and purposeful act of communication that is accomplished in a variety of environments, under various constraints of time, and with a variety of language resources and technological tools.
>
> —Definition of writing, National Center for Education Statistics (2012, p. 4)

The U.S. National Assessment of Educational Progress (NAEP) recently switched from a paper-and-pencil to a computer-based writing test. In 2011, the test was administered to a nationally representative sample of 8th- and 12th-grade students. Students were evaluated not only on their responses to questions and essays composed on laptop computers but on how frequently they used word-processing review tools, such as spell check, and editing tools, such as copying and cutting text. Some prompts also featured multimedia components. Results show only about one quarter of the students performed at the proficient level or higher, and the proficiency rates were far lower for Black and Hispanic students than their White counterparts (National Center for Education Statistics, 2012).

Digital writing is defined as "compositions created with, and oftentimes for reading or viewing on a computer or other devise that is connected to the Internet" (National Writing Project, 2010, p. 7). The change from a traditional paper-and-pencil writing environment to a digital one is profound in and of itself, as evidenced by the NAEP results. The good news is that the hallmarks of good writing instruction—teaching students the importance of the writing process and writing craft, and helping them analyze and understand the audience, purpose, context, and topic of their writing—remain the same in digital writing environments. However, what it means to live a literate life in the 21st century, and what it means to teach writers in contemporary contexts are important considerations for meaningful writing instruction. Hicks (2009) suggests that digital tools and environments can help teachers teach writing more effectively. These tools and environments promote not only understanding the *how* of writing but also the *intentional focus* of writing or the audience and purpose for which students are writing.

MODELS AND SUPPORTS FOR LEARNING TO WRITE ONLINE

Recently, I was in a meeting when one of my colleagues mentioned a *New York Times* article he had read online. Offhandedly, he said he had written a response to the article in the comments section. Then he leaned forward and said conspiratorially, "I just couldn't help myself!" I include this comment because I think it captures the interactive, collaborative, and participatory culture of the read/write web that makes it so engaging. As mentioned in other chapters, almost everything you read online offers a way to give feedback or to share it. You can comment, "like" or "not like," tweet, blog, bookmark, email, and so on.

The participatory nature of the read/write web extends the role of reader to creator, contributor, and distributor of knowledge to a worldwide audience. Participation is not defined by the tools but by the experience. Awareness of the audience and the possibility of global and/or peer response evoke the need for thoughtful reflection and critical thinking. For example, I was recently observing in a 3rd-grade classroom and working with a student who was writing an online book review. I asked him how it was going and, at first, he said fine. Then, he looked up at me and said, "I want this to be really good because my Grandma G in Arizona is going to read it and I know my friends will, too." He went back to working carefully, crafting and rereading his review with this very important audience in mind.

This same classroom afforded an example seen in Figure 7.1 of a new form and style of teacher to student interaction that can occur when teacher and student discussion of a book approaches that of peer readers' conversation about a book that both are reading.

In previous chapters, the way images, graphics, video, audio, and embedded links come together to broaden and deepen meaning when integrated effectively into prior knowledge were discussed. In this chapter, the reciprocity of using these media within the context of writing to communicate effectively and meaningfully will be discussed in addition to understanding the importance of audience and purpose for writing. As with reading, children need powerful models and supports for learning to communicate online.

Digital Mentor Texts and Media

Author and writing expert Katie Wood Ray (2004) believes that a sense of genre is what gives writers vision for writing. Therefore, you must plan for purposeful engagements that will immerse students in multiple genres—both traditional print-based and digital texts—and provide multiple opportunities for students to engage in and approximate digital reading and writing behaviors.

The use of mentor texts has become a prevalent method for showing students how a particular genre is structured. Ralph Fletcher (Sibberson, n.d.) states:

> I think mentor texts are any texts that you can learn from, and every writer, no matter how skilled you are or how beginning you are, encounters and reads something that can lift and inform and infuse their own writing.

Mentor texts provide students with opportunities to read, analyze, and emulate models of good writing and can serve as an anchor, or foundation, for students' writing. For traditional print-based writing, these texts are typically children's and young adult

**Figure 7.1. A 3rd-Grade Student's Blog Post About Reading and
His Teacher's Response**

literature (e.g., picture books and short chunks of text). It is just as important, however, to share with students exemplary examples of online writing and use of media.

Digital mentor texts and media should be exemplars, meaning they provide a clear, straightforward model for students. For example, the Wonderopolis site described in Chapter 4 provides a simple, clear example of how the use of an image can spark curiosity and provide a layer of understanding that text alone cannot. From a good example, teachers can conduct think-alouds, and students can then talk about the decision-making process for determining when the addition of a photograph or image will add meaning. This is really good critical thinking—thinking that teachers can capture on an anchor chart and use as a scaffold for students when they use these strategies in their own online writing.

Digital Anchor Charts

Anchor charts can be an effective scaffold for students' learning during modeled lessons. These charts, created by teachers and students, highlight specific guidelines or behaviors for performing a particular strategy, or serve as a concrete representation of students' thinking. Teachers can place these charts in the classroom where students can use them as a scaffold when beginning independent strategy use. There are a few issues, however, that make the use of anchor charts cumbersome or ineffective. Over time, these charts can become too numerous to display in the classroom, and, therefore, many teachers take them down, roll them up, and pull them back out when needed, which is time consuming. Also, the placement of the charts may prove difficult for some students to see.

Digital anchor charts follow the same guidelines as traditional anchor charts except they may be created in a digital environment such as a wiki, Google document, or blog post. Additionally, they document the guidelines for performing strategies modeled and discussed for digital writing. The fact that they can be made available to students electronically means that there are no drawbacks to the number of charts you create.

Evernote (www.evernote.com) is one online application that makes it easy to post these charts online so all students can access them anytime, anywhere. It is similar to an online notebook in which you can save almost anything from anywhere. Figure 7.2 shows a notebook for digital anchor charts. On the left side, all of the charts that have been saved are displayed and when one is selected, it is shown in the main frame. Photos of these charts were taken with a cell phone and sent directly to Evernote. Web-pages, emails, notes, images, links, text messages, scanned/PDF documents, videos, audio notes—almost anything can be sent to Evernote from a computer, iPad, or cell phone. Notebooks are created for each topic and items or "notes" such as each of the anchor charts in Figure 7.2 are stored within each notebook. You can also create audio or webcam notes in Evernote and post them to a notebook.

Pinterest (www.pinterest.com) and Learnist (www.learni.st/category/10-education) operate in a similar manner as Evernote except items are displayed differently. Figure 7.3 shows a Pinterest board for digital mentor texts. Items can be uploaded from a computer or sent from a cell phone and pinned to the board. There are a few differences between Evernote and Pinterest and Learnist when it comes to viewing webpages and media. One is that Pinterest and Learnist allow video and audio to be viewed/listened to directly in the application, whereas Evernote does not. When a media item is sent to Evernote, users must click on the link that will then go directly to the site. All of the sites allow teachers to quickly post an anchor chart so students can access it at school or at home. Digital anchor charts can serve as a guide for students' writing and multimedia composition, including response to reading, discussed in the next section.

DIGITAL READER RESPONSE

Reading comprehension involves the reader actively creating meaning by connecting the ideas in a text with his or her knowledge, beliefs, and experiences. This connection, or transaction, between text and reader is the premise of reader response (Rosenblatt, 1978). Though many things influence a reader's response (e.g., background knowledge, experiences), writing about a text provides a tool for visibly and permanently recording, connecting, analyzing, personalizing, and manipulating key ideas. In fact, recent research has shown that when students write about material they have read, it significantly enhances their reading comprehension. In the 2010 report, *Writing to Read: Evidence for How Writing Can Improve Reading*, Graham and Hebert shared the results of a meta-analysis of high quality research on writing techniques to enhance students' reading comprehension. The analysis found that extended writing about science, social studies, and language arts texts has a strong and consistently positive impact on reading comprehension. Specifically, reading comprehension improved when students wrote personal reactions and analyzed and interpreted the text over an extended period.

Figure 7.2. Evernote Notebook for Digital Anchor Charts

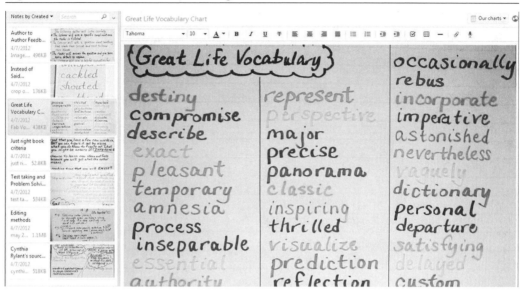

Figure 7.3. Pinterest Board for Digital Mentor Texts

Writing about texts that have been read was also found to be an effective activity for lower-achieving students (Graham & Hebert, 2010). However, Graham and Hebert advised caution, indicating that having lower-achieving students write about text without teaching them how to do so may not be effective. In other words, explicit instruction on how to respond in writing about reading is an important ingredient of improved comprehension.

How do teachers instruct students to write an effective response that is personal, analytical, and interpretive? (Of course, this will be different in the lower and upper grades.) Figure 7.4 shows an anchor chart created by a 3rd-grade teacher to support her students when responding to reading in a traditional reading response journal. Each box represents a comprehension strategy that had been modeled by the teacher, and practiced and used independently by the students. If students responded to reading from multiple categories on this chart, their responses would be personal, analytical, and interpretive.

Figure 7.4. Teacher-Created Anchor Chart with Criteria for Thoughtful Journal Entries

What Is a Thoughtful Response to Reading? **Making our thinking visible**	**Creates Mind Pictures/Visualizes** • How does the language (words, phrases) create visual or sensory images in my mind? • How does the author use language to create the setting/s? • How does the author use language to describe or create the character/s? • How does the author use text features to help me learn more about the topic?
Summarizes/Synthesizes • What are the important things I am learning or have learned from my reading? • What is the book mostly about? • What is the character like so far? • What do I think about what has happened so far? • What is the author trying to teach me?	**Makes Connections** • Does any part of the book remind me of my own life? • Does any part of the book remind me of the world and what is occurring or happened in the past? • Does any event, character or theme/ message remind me of another book? • Do I connect in any way with a character from the book?
Offers Opinion • Do I like or dislike the book? • Who is my favorite or least favorite character and why? • Will I read this book again? Why or why not? • Will I recommend this book to a friend? • Did this book teach me something? • What is my favorite part of the book and why?	**Critiques** • What are the resources the author uses to provide me with accurate and current information? • Did the author use text features to help me understand the information? • Did the author follow the text structures for the genre? • Do I agree or disagree with the way the author expressed meaning?

Figure 7.4. Teacher-Created Anchor Chart with Criteria for Thoughtful Journal Entries (continued)

Identifies Theme/Main Idea	Wondering, Making Predictions, and Inferences
• What is the author's message? • What did the message teach me? • How will the message change my life? • What is the text really about? • What did I learn from reading? • What more do I need to learn?	I wonder . . . I think . . . I know . . . because . . . What does _____ mean? The mood in the book is _____ so far.

Adapted from Dorn, L. & Soffos, C. (2005). *Teaching for deep comprehension: A reading workshop approach*. Portland, ME: Stenhouse.

What would you add to this chart to support students with writing a reading response online? Let's think about this by considering a brief blog post from Newbery Award-winning author Grace Lin (2011) in response to reading *Thimble Summer* (Enright, 1938). Lin's post included an image of the book's front cover, the publisher's summary, and the following response (underlining indicates hyperlinked text):

> *My Thoughts:* Another book that inspired my upcoming <u>Dumpling Days</u> (at one point the title was "The Dumpling Summer")! This is a sweet book that I always enjoyed, though I have had some interesting conversations with my friends about the <u>use of the word "fat"</u> in it. (Lin, 2011)

How is Lin's response on her blog different from what she might have written in a traditional paper journal? Table 7.1 compares the strategies she might have used in a traditional paper journal to those used to respond on her blog in terms of the following categories:

• Showing an awareness of audience, especially a worldwide audience
• Synthesizing information across multiple sources
• Evaluating the relevance of connections (i.e., links to other resources)
• Evaluating the relevance of additional images and media

It is easy to see, just from this brief example, that writing online requires the reader's response to include not only the same level of personal connections, analysis, and interpretation as traditional response formats but additional higher order thinking skills. To fully understand and use these additional skills, students must be able to see them modeled, practice them with support, and use them independently. The following sections discuss ways to engage students in online written response to reading.

Table 7.1. Comparison of Strategies Grace Lin Used for Response to _Thimble Summer_ in a Traditional Paper versus Online Environment

Strategies needed for online writing	Traditional Paper Journal	Blog
Awareness of audience, especially a worldwide audience	Lin would have written about how the book influenced her own writing, but probably would not have included the title of her own book or the book she had just read.	Lin included the title of her book, and the book she had just read because otherwise, a worldwide audience might not know what she was talking about and it also made a personal connection.
Synthesizing information across multiple sources	Lin probably would have indicated that she enjoyed the book and thought it was sweet, and what she thought about the author's use of the word "fat." She probably would not have included her conversation with friends.	Lin hyperlinks the word "fat" to another blog post (for which she is one of several contributors) that further discusses the use of the word "fat" in the book.
Evaluating the relevance of connections (i.e., links to other resources)		Lin linked _Thimble Summer_ (Enright, 1938) to an online bookstore so readers who may not know about this book could learn more or even purchase it. She also linked to the discussion of the word "fat" on another blog. The decision to provide these links was based on relevance to the audience and trustworthiness of the sites to which they were linked.
Evaluating the relevance of additional images and media		Lin included an image of _Thimble Summer_ in her post, which added another layer of information for the reader.

Blogs as Response Journals

Blogs provide an easy and natural transition from paper-and-pencil response activities to online writing environments because they are easy to use and intuitive. The first step is to become familiar with other teacher/class blogs. You might want to start with the Scholastic article *Top 20 Teacher Blogs* (www.scholastic.com/teachers/article/ top-20-teacher-blogs). As you peruse other teachers' blogs, consider the features you like such as ease of use and display.

Create a class blog on which all students may respond to reading. Blogmeister (www.classblogmeister.com), Kidblog (www.kidblog.org/home), and Blogger (www. blogger.com) are just some of the many free blog sites. If you're not a blogger already, take the time to learn how to use the tools on whichever site you choose. Settings will allow teachers to make the blog private or public or to make commenting available.

Writing responses online should build on students' prior knowledge of how to respond to reading in thoughtful and meaningful ways that deepen their comprehension, as well as appreciation of and connections with text. If students do not have this foundational understanding, they will not be able to employ the higher order thinking skills and strategies of writing with audience awareness and purpose in mind, and synthesizing and evaluating that make online responses meaningful. Begin with what students know and slowly introduce new strategies for online writing. The guidelines that make up the remainder of this section will help teachers do so.

Begin with writing a traditional response to reading. Conduct several lessons modeling how to write a traditional response to a class read-aloud, allowing students to participate in constructing the response with you. Stress the importance of using the writing process and correct use of conventions, since it ultimately affects the creditability of the blogger. Use these posts as digital anchor charts for students to use for their own writing.

Next, use digital mentor texts. Show students exemplary blog posts that were written in response to reading. In addition to Grace Lin, who blogs reading responses via weekly posts titled "book talks," many children's authors have blogs on which they write about books they are reading.

Slowly introduce and model strategies unique to writing responses online:

- using audience awareness to decide what to include in the response
- deciding whether to include an image or other multimedia to support a response to reading
- determining whether to link to other information such as the author's blog, a book reviewer's blog, other students' blogs, or other online resources
- synthesizing what has been learned from reading the blog responses of classmates, and including or referencing that information in a response or comment

Together, create a rubric for blog responses so each student understands the expectations. Then post the rubric with the digital anchor charts and mentor texts. For an example of a blog rubric, see: langwitches.org/blog/wp-content/uploads/2012/04/ blogging-commenting-rubric.pdf.

Assign blog partners who are required to comment on each other's blog posts to ensure that everyone receives comments. Blog partners can change over time.

Consider expanding the audience—and the possibility of receiving comments from around the world—by making the blog public or at least visible to parents. This shift in audience from the teacher to the class to the world fundamentally changes students' motivation and engagement. That said, teach students about the importance of remaining anonymous online.

As students become more adept at writing blog responses, introduce the use of new media for reading response, such as podcasting and video. Young adult author John Green (www.nerdfighters.ning.com) often uses video blogging (vlog: a video posted on a blog). A few years ago, a school district attempted to ban his Printz Award-winning book *Looking for Alaska* (2005), which includes an awkward sexual scene between two teenagers that the district considered obscene. Green posted a vlog (www.youtube.com/watch?v=fHMPtYvZ8tM) that was a passionate appeal for why the scene was important to the book and, in this context, should not be considered obscene. Green's vlog was more powerful than a written message would have been because the viewer could hear and see his passion regarding the issue.

IRT LESSON FOR YOUNGER STUDENTS: HOW TO CONSTRUCT BLOG POSTS

Phase 1: Teacher modeling

Step 1: Planning the lesson. You will need:

- chart paper
- sticky notes
- a prepared personal response to reading

This lesson will assist younger students with understanding the importance of considering audience awareness when writing an online response to reading. The modeling phase of the lesson employs the write-aloud approach to model a traditional journal response to reading that will be written on a piece of chart paper. Writing aloud, or modeled writing, is a strategy in which teachers think aloud as they compose a piece of writing in front of students, making the *writing process* visible and concrete. The IRTs in this chapter do not require the use of technology; they do, however, require reading comprehension, writing, categorizing, analyzing, reflecting, evaluating, synthesizing, and working collaboratively. The students will then be able to transfer these skills to a digital medium.

To elicit an authentic response from students, write a personal response to a book that most children in the class haven't read. Afterward, give students sticky notes on which they will ask questions about your response or about the book that were not answered in your response. For example, I recently read *Amelia Lost: The Life and Disappearance of Amelia Earhart* (Fleming, 2011). If I were writing a personal response to this book in a journal, I might write the following:

This book was fascinating! I thought I knew a lot about Amelia Earhart until I read *Amelia Lost* by Candice Fleming. It was written in a unique format that moved back and forth between her childhood and her famous last flight. This prompted me to think about how her childhood and events in her life contributed to her decision to make the flight from which she would never return. I think the most interesting information I learned was that there were many people who tried to help Amelia after her plane disappeared.

What questions do you have after reading this response? Maybe you don't know the story of Amelia Earhart and you are curious to learn more. What was the "famous last flight" on which her plane apparently disappeared? Did you wonder what Amelia Earhart looked like or what the format of the book looked like? Did you wonder why the author wrote the book in that format or why she wrote the book in the first place? Did you wonder about the people who tried to help Earhart? Students might have all these questions and more.

Step 2: Introduce the lesson. Tell students that you are going to think aloud while you model the process of writing a personal response to a book you just read. Ask students to listen carefully and think about the decisions you make about the information to include in the response.

Step 3: Model the process. Model the process of writing your personal response. Using the write-aloud process, demonstrate your decisionmaking process for determining what to include in your response (i.e., teacher-student created rubric discussed in the previous section).

When the write-aloud is complete, ask students if they have questions about the book or your response. Ask students to share their questions with a partner.

Give each student or pair of students two or three sticky notes. Ask them to write their questions on the notes. When finished, ask students to stick the notes on the chart paper.

Read aloud several students' questions. Ask students why they think there were so many questions. Discuss how your response was based on your knowledge and you didn't think about the information the students may need for the response to be meaningful to them. Make the point that writing for a specific audience requires writers to think about the information the audience might need or want and to include it in their response.

Phase 2: Teacher and student demonstrations

Categorizing information: Together, categorize the questions into the types of information requested (background information on the book, information about the author, etc.). Read each question aloud and categorize accordingly.

Analyzing information: When the questions are categorized, ask students to discuss additional information that might be necessary to make a response meaningful for a worldwide audience.

Phase 3: Independent practice

Generating information: Organize students into small groups of three to four students. Ask each student to read aloud one of his or her own reading responses and the other group members to ask questions that would help the students think about additional information that would make the response meaningful for everyone.

Evaluating information: Ask each group to consider whether the additional information would help or distract the reader.

Synthesizing information: Ask all students to rewrite their responses, including the new information that the groups indicated would be helpful.

IRT LESSON FOR OLDER STUDENTS: HOW TO LINK TO ADDITIONAL INFORMATION

Phase 1: Teacher modeling

Step 1: Planning the lesson. You will need:

- chart paper
- a prepared personal response to reading
- knowledge of web resources with additional information that supports reader response

This lesson is meant to assist older readers with understanding—and appreciating—how blogs allow writers to make connections to lots of information that might be informative to readers while keeping the length of the blog post itself relatively intact. Keep in mind: It is impossible to include all the information that *every* reader may need without turning a personal response into an informative essay. Let's return to the response about *Amelia Lost* (Fleming, 2011). Many students would probably want to know more about Amelia Earhart, but it would take a lot of additional information to explain her famous flight. Rather than include all this information in the blog post, the writer could provide a link to a website about her. Those people who want to know more could click the link and those that don't could read on.

Determining whether to provide links to information and/or to include that information in the blog post requires the writer to think about the text and its audience in critical ways:

- Does the link provide access to important information that will support the reader or does it take the reader off task?
- If the readers don't click the link, will they still understand the response?
- What types of media can be linked or embedded, and what is the potential of these different types of media to inform the reader?
- Is the linked information valid and reliable?

Each of these questions could constitute a lesson in and of itself; however, this IRT focuses on the initial purpose and decision of whether to include a link or links to support the reader. However, the ability to link information assumes that students will have access to the Internet to research supporting resources and understands how to determine if resources are valid and reliable (see Chapter 8).

Step 2: Introduce the lesson. Tell students they are going to learn about linking information in blog posts. Explain that this is a strategic process that requires the writer to think critically about the audience and the information being linked. Indicate that you are going to model the process, and students should listen carefully and think about the questions you are asking and the decisions you are making to determine what and when to link.

Step 3: Model the process. Note: For this step, *Amelia Lost* (Fleming, 2011) will be used as an example. Using chart paper, display your reading response and read it aloud. Model the decisionmaking process by thinking aloud about the information that might be helpful to a reader unfamiliar with Amelia Earhart. For example, you might tell students:

> If anyone reading my response is unfamiliar with Amelia Earhart, more information about her would be very helpful. However, it would take a lot of information to tell the story of Amelia Earhart, and the purpose of my blog post is to share my thoughts about the book, not Amelia Earhart. So if I provide a link to a valid and reliable website about Amelia Earhart, readers who need or want more information can click the link. Those who don't may read on.

Model when and where to include the link (see Figure 7.5). Indicate that you are including the link in the very beginning of your response so readers have the option of learning more before reading on. Underline *Amelia Earhart* in the first sentence of the response and indicate that her name will link to a website with information about her. Explain that you are only linking Earhart's name, rather than the entire sentence, so the reader can easily infer the exact information the link provides.

Continue to model the decisionmaking process. As you read on, demonstrate one or more questions of the decisionmaking process for including links.

Phase 2: Teacher and student demonstrations

Generate questions. Request permission from a student to use his or her written book response as an example. Organize students into groups of three to four, and ask them to read the response and generate questions they may have about it.

Analyze questions. Ask several groups to share one of their questions with the class. Then as a class or in groups, discuss what additional information will be necessary to answer each question.

Evaluate questions. Discuss with students whether the information required to answer each question will support or distract the reader.

Figure 7.5. Response to *Amelia Lost* with links

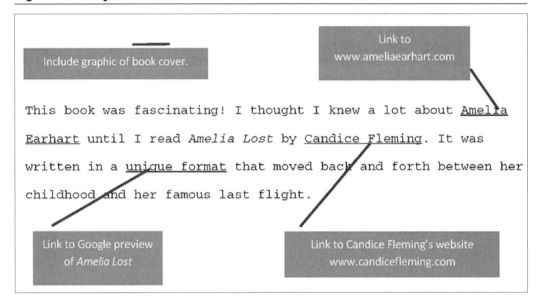

Determine when and where to include the link. Once important information has been determined, ask students to discuss in groups when and where would be the most appropriate place in the response to provide a link to additional information.

Phase 3: Independent practice

Ask students to repeat the lesson activity using one of their own book responses. When all students are finished, share with each other in partners or groups.

Follow-up activities:

- ***Create links to include in blog responses.*** Each blog provider uses a different way to create links; however, this process is usually very easy and intuitive. Modeling the process and providing opportunities for students to practice shouldn't take more than one or two lessons.

Embed Media within a Blog Response

Including videos or podcasts in (or as) a response requires strategic thinking about the audience and the information conveyed through media as opposed to other digital resources such as websites. For example, in the previous IRT for older students, the teacher-modeled reading response includes a link to Candice Fleming's website for readers who want to know more about her. On the author's website is a video of Fleming discussing why she chooses to research and write about prominent historical figures. Perhaps this video could have been embedded in the blog response so that a reader could watch the video on the blog. The critical part of making the decision to embed the video is its importance to the post. Though the video provides good information on the author's reasoning and research process, the teacher decided this was tangential to the purpose of her post. By providing a link to the author's website, interested readers can find out more, but embedding the video takes the reader away from the intent of the post.

On the other hand, there is a preview of the book available through Google Books (books.google.com/books?id=xLDMzDAdPREC&lpg=PP1&pg=PP1#v=onepage&q&f=false) that can be embedded in the blog that would allow readers to see the interesting and engaging format of the book. The teacher decided to embed this preview on the blog. Modeling and engaging students in this type of critical reasoning is important work.

Commenting on Blog Posts

As mentioned at the beginning of this chapter, readers can respond to almost everything they read online, which supports the interactive, collaborative, and participatory nature of the read/write web. It also motivates and engages students. However, students must understand that with this opportunity to respond comes responsibility to do so appropriately.

Have you ever left a comment or read the comments of others for any type of online content? If so, you probably noted the wide range in the types and quality of comments. Often, the lines have become blurred between the quick, brief, shorthand responses of texting and tweeting and the more conventional forms of written response. Just as in most traditional forms of writing, the use of writing conventions, emoticons, and abbreviations in digital writing is acceptable in more informal, social situations and inappropriate in more formal, academic settings. "This iz so rad!!!!!!!" may be an appropriate response to a friend's Facebook post, but not a *New York Times* online article. The difference between the two: purpose and audience.

Students often come into classrooms having only observed or participated in social commenting; after all, the use of social media to stay in contact with relatives or friends is the predominant way many adults and older siblings in a child's life interact with the Internet. Children are eager to emulate this behavior, and it is natural for them to want to interact socially with their classmates. That is another reason it is important to provide opportunities for students to learn about and interact with one another through classroom community-building activities such as those described in Chapter 3. The more students know about one another, the more connections they will be able to make when discussing their reading. Students must understand that the purpose of commenting is to contribute thoughtfully and meaningfully to a conversation with the author and other readers of the post.

As with blogging, the first step to assisting students with how to construct a quality comment is to become familiar with comments on other blogs to get a sense of the range of comments. Once you have found several quality responses, consider using them as digital mentor texts for students. You will also want to explore the settings on the blog you are using. Options are available for restricting who can comment, where the comment section appears on the blog, and comment moderation (comments must be approved by the blog owner before being published).

Conducting IRT lessons on commenting that model, demonstrate, and engage students in thinking about and writing quality comments is essential. Consider the guidelines in Table 7.2 to help students create meaningful, thoughtful comments.

Model writing or sharing comments you have made on students' blogs and share mentor text comments. Create class commenting guidelines and add to digital anchor charts. Then, consider conducting an IRT lesson using *paper* comments; that is, write a blog post on chart paper and ask students to "comment" using sticky notes. Engage students in thinking through their comments with the following questions:

- Was there evidence of understanding and reflection on the content of the blog post?
- Did it contribute to the topic of the blog post?
- Was there a meaningful addition (information, idea, perspective, connection, question)?
- Did the comment add links to additional relevant resources?

DIGITAL WRITING WORKSHOP

Writing in response to reading, as discussed in the first part of this chapter, requires students to respond, analyze, and interpret a text written by someone else. However, students must also learn to compose their own writing across genres. Teaching students the writing process is effective in helping students learn to write well and to use writing as a tool for learning (Graham & Perin, 2007). A process-writing approach in a traditional workshop environment stresses strategy instruction in a number of writing instructional activities such as:

- minilessons
- extended writing opportunities
- writing for authentic audiences
- collaborative writing and peer editing
- personalized instruction through conferencing
- cycles of writing

Digital writing workshop integrates new literacies and digital writing tools into the teaching of the writing process (Hicks, 2009).

The following sections describe ways in which digital environments can support learning and collaboration within specific elements of a writing workshop.

Digital Writer's Notebook

Why do writers write? Consider my son. He always carries a small notebook in his back pocket so he is able to capture something he sees or hears that sparks a writing idea. The freedom to write about whatever they are curious about or find interesting is the basis for why writers write. Giving students a choice in what they write—topics,

Table 7.2. Guidelines to Help Students Create Meaningful and Thoughtful Blog Comments

- Focus on the content of the post and react as you read.
- Confirm the author's good thinking and ask questions to clarify misunderstandings.
- Relate the connections you are making to what the author has posted.
- Think about what you would say to the author if you were conversing with him or her about the post.
- Think about the author's perspective and relate your own.
- Consider what further information you would like to know. For example, would it be beneficial for the author to provide examples or evidence from the text?
- Share additional helpful information about the topic via linked resources. For example, do you know of other books the author might like that are similar or about the same topic?

genres, styles—is at the heart of a writing workshop approach. Students may get ideas during minilessons, from classmates or from everyday experiences, and a notebook is a place where a writer can collect ideas for writing, write to think about ideas, rehearse ideas and textual forms, try out ideas that might end up in drafts, and develop initial ideas into more extended text.

I am a writer, too, but unlike my son, I carry a camera to collect my ideas. I have an application on my phone for Evernote, discussed earlier in this chapter. If I see something that sparks a writing idea, I take a picture and send it to my online writer's notebook. Evernote allows me to capture my ideas in forms other than pictures, too. I can capture text, websites, video, audio—almost anything anywhere from my phone or computer. Evernote, Pinterest, and other similar applications extend the boundaries of the writer's notebook, which is handy since ideas don't just develop in a classroom where a student writer's notebook lives. Students can easily share their collection of ideas with one another.

Prewriting

Student engagement in prewriting activities has been shown to have consistently positive effects on the quality of students' writing (Cunningham & Cunningham, 2010). However, these activities do not need to be elaborate or time consuming. Brainstorming, clustering, mind mapping, and webbing are quick visual ways of generating a lot of information about a topic by building on the association of terms or exploring the relationships between ideas. Several online visual tools allow students to brainstorm or explore ideas and then make connections by linking similarly themed words or ideas.

SpiderScribe (www.spiderscribe.net) is a mind map creation tool that can be used individually or collaboratively. Users can add images, maps, calendars, text notes, and uploaded text files to their mind maps. These elements can stand alone or be connected. SpiderScribe mind maps can be embedded into a blog or website. Other sites such as bubbl.us (www.bubbl.us) and Slatebox (www.slatebox.com) provide online mapping tools that display students' ideas. Slatebox also allows students to embed photos into their maps, save maps and embed them in a blog or other online source, and collaborate with others by sharing a link to the map (see Figure 7.6).

Collaborative Writing, Peer Editing, and Publishing

Collaborative writing is a research-based practice for effective writing instruction (Graham & Perin, 2007), that uses instructional arrangements in which students work together to plan, draft, revise, and edit their writing. In many classrooms, writing is a solitary activity, yet interaction and dialogue with others is crucial for learning. Conversations with a partner can stimulate and modify thoughts and ideas. Many critically acclaimed, award-winning authors have cited their participation in a writing group as a major reason for their success. For example, Jane Yolen writes of her group, "As for their critiques—they have saved me from overwriting, underwriting, and no writing. They have encouraged me and instilled courage in me when I needed it" (Yolen, n.d.).

Collaboration changes how people view and understand their contributions in any project. Suddenly, it is not the individual's work that is most valued, but that of the team. Yet the individual's work remains a necessary part of the whole. Without each competently developed part, the whole suffers. In a society where ideas are highly valued, learning to create and share together is critical.

In the classroom, peers provide specific, thoughtful, and meaningful comments on their classmates' work, whereas teachers tend to do more correcting. This collaborative process also helps students to develop analytical and critical thinking skills and better judge their own writing. The ability to collaborate is an important 21st-century skill, as

Figure 7.6. Idea Map Created with Slatebox

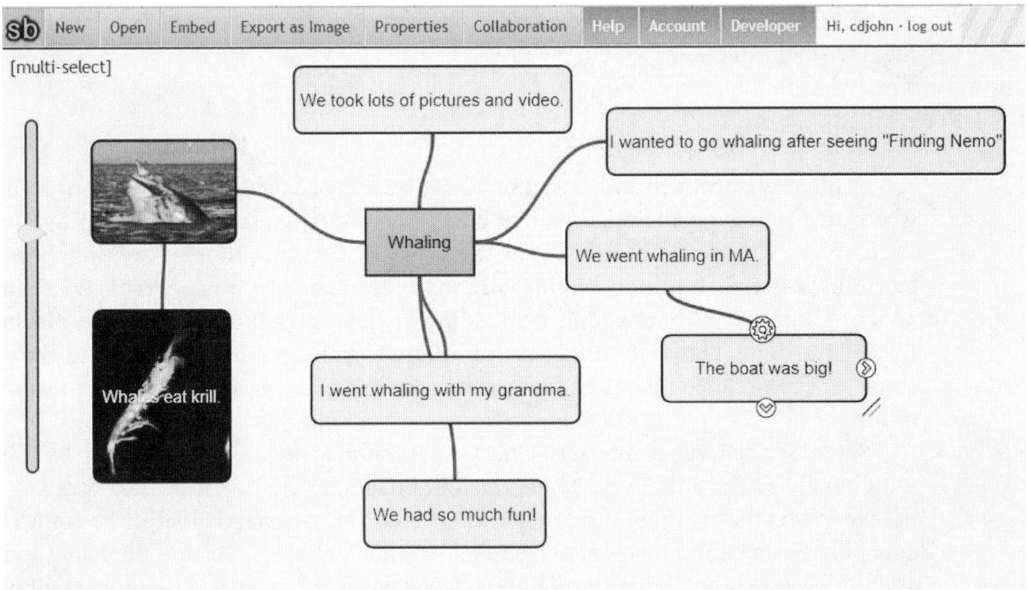

evidenced by the many digital environments that support and promote opportunities for collaboration.

Collaborative writing in a digital environment allows students to draw from the strengths of a diverse class or small group. Some students may have keen critical thinking skills and others may be organizational wizards or shine at adding details. Through collaborative writing, students benefit from recognizing and learning from the strengths of their classmates. Additionally, students benefit from peer review and peer editing as they complete writing projects. The increase in telecommuting has prompted the need for employees to collaborate virtually on writing tasks in the form of team projects, preparing reports, and making presentations. Therefore, providing students opportunities to work together and problem solve while providing effective writing instruction can prepare students for their literacy futures.

Collaborative storytelling involves two or more writers working together on a story or one writer starting the story while others add threads to it. Several tools allow students to write collaboratively, from basic shared writing spaces to more structured environments, but all provide access from anywhere, anytime, and allow multiple collaborators.

Google Docs (www.google.com/docs) is an online word processor that lets students create and format text documents, and collaborate with other people in real time. Students can invite others to collaborate on a writing piece, giving them edit, comment, or view access. Students and teachers can view the document's revision history and roll back to any previous version. Google Docs can be saved to a computer in a number of formats and can be translated to different languages.

A wiki is a website developed collaboratively by a community of users, allowing any user to add and edit content. It has the same advantages of Google Docs, including the familiarity of a word processor, but with the addition of the characteristics of a webpage. A "history" button allows users to see changes over time. Teachers can create a wiki for collaborative writing on any of the free wiki sites such as Wikispaces (www.wikispaces.com), or Wikistory (www.wikistory.com), which is dedicated to collaborative story writing and offers the opportunity to join in a space in which many other authors are writing.

VoiceThread, discussed in Chapter 3, is a great tool for sharing student writing. Students can upload their documents and record themselves reading their stories, and their classmates can record or write comments.

Zopler (www.zopler.com) provides a more structured way for students to collaborate on their writing. One student starts a story or brainstorms ideas about a topic. Then other students can add to the story, topic, or idea. In addition, students can upload pictures and vote on one another's writing.

MixedInk (www.mixedink.com) also provides a structured approach to collaborative writing. The process is presented in Figure 7.7.

Students can comment on one another's drafts and add words and language from another student's writing to their own writing. MixedInk takes the highest rated parts of students' stories and remixes them to create a new text. Automatic authorship tracking displays original authorship with color-coded text as students appropriate their peers' work.

Figure 7.7. MixedInk's Collaborative Writing Structure

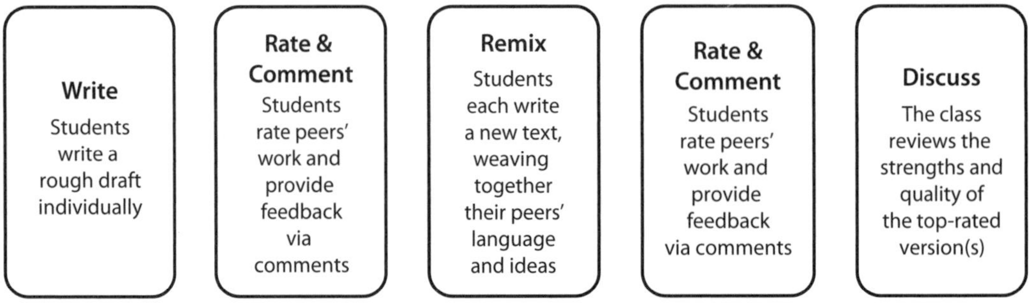

Write	Rate & Comment	Remix	Rate & Comment	Discuss
Students write a rough draft individually	Students rate peers' work and provide feedback via comments	Students each write a new text, weaving together their peers' language and ideas	Students rate peers' work and provide feedback via comments	The class reviews the strengths and quality of the top-rated version(s)

Source: www.mixedink.com/userguide.pdf (p. 1).

Storybird (www.storybird.com) reverses the process of visual storytelling by starting with the image. Students can choose a theme with a predesigned template and use it as a backdrop of the story or content or select from dozens of images to create their own story. Students can collaborate on a story or take turns, adding more words and pictures either sitting side-by-side or at different times. The completed story is published as an online book and can be shared with others. Students can create a library of books written by other students so they are sharing their stories with each other.

ZooBurst (www.zooburst.com) is a digital environment in which students can create 3D books. Students can arrange characters and props within a 3D world that they can customize using artwork found in a built-in database of over 10,000 free images and materials. ZooBurst authors can share books with readers using a simple hyperlink, and books can easily be embedded in any website or blog, allowing authors to provide their own contextual framework to their stories. Students can also moderate a discussion forum for each book, providing a virtual space in which readers can interact with one another.

There are two online resources for creating comic strips: Make Beliefs Comix (www.makebeliefscomix.com) and Comic Creator (www.readwritethink.org/files/resources/interactives/comic/index.html). Students select from the sites' provided elements to choose a person or thing that will be the focus of the story, add props, backgrounds and speech bubbles to create the comic. Both follow similar formats, although Make Beliefs Comix offers a few more choices for graphics and also allows students to write in seven different languages. Neither program allows students to save the finished product online so they must be printed.

CHAPTER 8

Technology Across the Curriculum

Wonder brings respect, energy, and determination to our work.

—Andrea Smith (2011), 3rd- and 4th-grade multi-age teacher

In Linda Urban's children's book, *The Center of Everything* (2013), 5th-grader Nero DeNiro gets into a lot of trouble with his teachers for asking too many questions. In the excerpt that follows, his friend Ruby reflects on the situation after Nero asks her several "crazy questions":

> This is exactly the kind of question that gets Nero DeNiro in so much trouble at school— the kind of question that teachers can't answer. A couple of teachers liked Nero for it. Mr. Cipielewski, in particular, thought Nero's questions showed an active and creative mind, but even he had to keep Nero in line, because otherwise they would never get through all the day's materials, and then when it was time for the assessment tests, it would look like his students hadn't learned anything, even though they had learned many amazing non-assessable things. (p. 96)

This fictional classroom scene resonates with most teachers. The ever present accountability for teaching the curriculum and assessing students' knowledge of that curriculum seems to present an either/or scenario: Either teach students the information that will be tested or allow them to go off on tangents that risk them not passing the test. The crux, however, is not *whether* teachers teach the curriculum, but *how* they teach it. It seems that the fundamental shift lies in understanding that studying academic content is a means of developing competencies rather than the goal—in seeing students as learners as opposed to knowers. In other words, students must be problem posers as well as problem solvers, and problem posing begins with asking questions.

Children enter school with unbound imagination, curiosity, and creativity across the disciplines. Over time, however, many come to believe that knowing the right answer is far more important than asking thoughtful questions. As it turns out, the most important skill needed to excel in the information-based job market of today is the ability to ask good "nonassessable" questions. Harvey and Goudvis (2013) write:

> Reading, writing, and thinking across disciplines promotes literacy in the broadest sense of the term. We'd argue that our democracy depends on making sure our kids build their knowledge store about the world so they are prepared to read with a critical eye and a skeptical stance. They [Students] need to sift, sort, and evaluate the barrage of information

that bombards them each and every day. They can't swallow whole everything they read, view, and hear. They need to be ready, willing, and eager to engage in dialogue—with their peers, their elders, their bosses, and, while still in school, their teachers. And above all, they must continually ask questions to become informed, engaged, and thoughtful citizens. (p. 439)

In his 2008 book *The Global Achievement Gap*, Wagner situates U.S. school problems in the larger context of the demands of the global knowledge economy. With insights gained from visits to classrooms in leading suburban schools throughout the United States, he analyzed student performance by considering the skills they will need to get a good job and become a productive citizen:

The habit of asking good questions was most frequently mentioned as an essential component of critical-thinking and problem-solving skills. It turns out that asking good questions, critical thinking, and problem solving go hand in hand in the minds of most employers and business consultants, and taken together they represent the First Survival Skill of the new global "knowledge economy." (p. 15)

LEARNING TO ASK QUESTIONS

Kelm (2005) believes there are no neutral questions, since "Every inquiry takes us somewhere, even if it is back to what we originally believed. Inhabiting this spirit of wonder can transform our lives, and the unconditional positive question is one of the greatest tools we have to this end" (p. 54). Students who learn to ask questions and inquire into academic content continue to be stimulated by new information and ideas as adults. Additionally, questioning is an aspect of critical thinking that is necessary to be an active and informed citizen in an information-based society.

My son is a good example of inquiry leading to expertise from childhood into adulthood. At an early age, he was interested in photography. There were no photography courses in his middle or high school, so when we bought him a camera for his 16th birthday, he began to learn on his own through self-study and trial and error. He took thousands of pictures and became interested in the variables that affected the composition and quality of his photos. He studied the camera's manual, watched numerous YouTube tutorials, downloaded editing software, posted photos to his Facebook and Tumblr sites, talked with friends who were also interested in photography, and joined online photography groups. He went to college to become a writer but found himself continually drawn to photography and videography. He volunteered for internships with photographers and magazines, shared his work on his Vimeo site and other social media, such as Instagram and Twitter, and continued to develop his editing skills on professional software such as Final Cut Pro and Photoshop. His photos and videos have been seen by millions of people in *Vogue* and *Fiasco* magazines and on websites, and he has won competitions and received awards—all with no traditional classroom instruction.

An important aspect of my son's story is that his curiosity about photography started in elementary school. His 4th-grade teacher was passionate about Civil War history. In addition to reading content in the social studies textbook, his teacher read aloud many picture books and shared primary sources of information. She then invited the students to choose an aspect of the Civil War that interested them and to work in groups to conduct further research. My son was captivated by the photographs in the books and primary source documents. How did they take pictures then? Who took the pictures and why? Just think how much he had to learn about the Civil War and then apply that knowledge to the particular context of photography to answer his questions!

To scaffold students' capacity to ask questions within the context of academic content, teachers must first *engage and motivate* students with content, sparking curiosity to pose questions that prompt deeper thinking and further investigation. Then, students must have access to *information and expertise* about the content being studied. Finally, students must learn how to use *critical thinking* to connect their own interests to the content in a way that results in good questioning. Each of the components that lead to asking good questions—engagement and motivation, information and expertise, and critical thinking—will only flourish in a classroom environment that embraces problem solving and problem posing, collaboration, and exploration. The following sections take a closer look at each component.

Engagement and Motivation

Students often see information books as a series of facts rather than a way to explore ideas. As such, they see content-area reading as a way to learn new information or facts rather than a way to enrich, expand, and illuminate a sense of wonder and curiosity. Teachers can do much to change this perception by displaying their own interest in content material and encouraging students to make personal connections to content material.

Teachers have a profound influence on student learning. Recent research by Mazer (2013) found that a teacher's immediacy and clarity positively impacts students in ways that have immediate and long-lasting effects on students' interest and engagement. Immediacy factors include verbal and nonverbal behaviors that generate perceptions of closeness between the teacher and students, including the use of eye contact, movement, facial expressions, and vocal variety. Teacher clarity behaviors can increase cognitive interest because they make information more organized and understandable for students. Verbal behaviors may include teacher talk about course material, and nonverbal behavior may include the use of graphic organizers, handouts, and notes. Thus, by modeling yourself as interested, excited, and curious about academic content and by modeling how you organize, understand, and ask questions about the material, teachers increase the likelihood of students becoming interested and engaged in content learning.

Teachers often encourage students to respond to fiction texts with personal connections and interpretations. When interpreting texts, students create their own meaning through a *transaction* with the text, since all readers bring their own emotions, concerns, life experiences, and knowledge to their reading. Teachers often use text-to-self, text-to-text, and text-to-world strategies as a way to prompt students to make these important connections. However, when it comes to nonfiction, aesthetic response to reading usually stops (Rosenblatt, 1978). It seems that the facts are the facts, and emotions, concerns, life experiences, and knowledge no longer play a role. This, of course, is not true: Students often impose their own knowledge on a text without reading attentively to see if their prior knowledge matches what the author is saying. Allowing children to respond to nonfiction not only exposes inaccuracies in prior knowledge but prompts students' sense of wonder and curiosity, which in turn prompts further learning.

Information and Expertise

Expertise, or knowledge, about a subject, often comes from a content-area textbook. Textbooks are essential but limited classroom tools for conveying content-area curriculum. Content-area textbooks are limited because they are often written well above grade level, not reader friendly (i.e., poor layout such as graphics and images not corresponding with the supporting text), outdated, and shallow in depth and breadth on any given topic. Teachers can do much to ameliorate this situation by demonstrating skills and strategies for reading a textbook effectively and by bringing in other sources of information such as trade books, magazines, primary source documents, online resources, and outside experts. These additional resources also promote excitement and engagement in the content and serve as resources for continued inquiry.

Critical Thinking

Though motivation to learn and access to multiple sources of information about content are two huge components of problem solving, knowing how to connect the two in ways that result in asking good questions and posing new problems takes critical thinking. Critical thinking is dependent on comprehension of the text but moves beyond basic comprehension to inferring, applying, analyzing, synthesizing, and evaluating information that guides deeper understanding and inquiry.

The ability to think critically can happen at all ages and developmental levels. As cognitive psychologist Daniel Willingham (2007) states, "It is a type of thought that even 3-year-olds can engage in—and even trained scientists can fail in" (p. 10). This is because critical thinking is not a set of skills that can be deployed at any time, in any context. It is dependent on subject-area knowledge and practice.

Some ideas for scaffolding critical thinking in the classroom when reading, writing, and thinking about content area learning are as follows:

- Introduce a concept and ask questions that draw from students' everyday knowledge and experiences.
- Model critical thinking strategies for students and allow students to practice using them independently.
- Create anchor charts that label and provide different examples of a particular strategy that can be used as a guide for ongoing practice.
- Provide opportunities for students to engage in conversations around content in a manner similar to book clubs. Discussion and debate among classmates provides multiple perspectives on content to create more insights and questions.
- Offer opportunities for students to engage in reading, listening, and viewing multiple sources of information on a topic. Then use graphic organizers or frames to help students look at the information in multiple ways.

- Promote questioning the author/text as the authority: Invite students to think of the text as a jumping off point to learn more or to think of different interpretations, applications, and innovations on the content.

INQUIRY LEARNING

Inquiry learning is not a method of teaching science, history, or any other subject, but "a stance toward experiences and ideas—a willingness to wonder, to ask questions, and to seek to understand by collaborating with others in the attempt to make answers to them" (Wells, 1999, p. 121). Thus, inquiry is a disposition that influences the way in which all classroom activities are approached.

Hattie's synthesis of over 800 meta-analyses relating to achievement showed that inquiry-based instruction produced "transferrable critical thinking skills as well as significant domain benefits, improved achievement, and improved attitude toward the subject" (Hattie, 2009, pp. 209–210). Indeed, after a decade of research in elementary classrooms, Allington and Johnston (2002) found that exemplary teachers encourage their students to view themselves as researchers and to approach learning through inquiry.

Teacher effectiveness coach Leslie Maniotes (as cited in Swartz, 2013) states, "We want [children] reflecting on the process and the content. Inquiry learning works best on longer, deep dive projects when students have to create something of their own out of what they've found" (paragraph 2). Maniotes has found that students need the following tools to guide inquiry learning:

- Inquiry Community/Circle: Each member of the class is a part of the inquiry community, exploring a topic related to the same class unit. A small inquiry circle of students can help one another explore and clarify ideas.
- Inquiry Journal/Log: This is a place for students to reflect on both the process and the content as they inquire into their topic of interest, documenting the process and product of research.
- Inquiry Chart: This tool helps students identify and visualize a central question by brainstorming and mapping their ideas in many ways.

Used in tandem, these tools can help students dig deeper into the inquiry process and gain insight into their own learning (Swartz, 2013). Along the way, students must infer, apply, analyze, synthesize, and evaluate multiple forms and sources of information while observing, collaborating, and experimenting with peers, teachers, and other resources outside of school. Many online tools can assist students with researching, documenting, and sharing their inquiry processes and products.

Internet Inquiry

Wagner (2008) writes:

> The real literacy of tomorrow entails the ability to be your own personal reference librarian—to know how to navigate through confusing, complex information spaces and feel

comfortable doing so. Navigation may well be the main form of literacy for the 21st century. (p. 179)

Today's youth are media situated but not media literate—using multimedia doesn't mean that students have developed the ability to understand the media and think critically about what they are experiencing (Ito et al., 2013).

To find websites that support their research and interests, students must learn how to use a web browser to conduct a search. This is essential since a haphazard approach to finding information can lead to frustration. The skills and strategies for conducting a productive search are unique to the Internet. Henry (2006) suggests the SEARCH framework for teaching students how to search for information on the Internet, which involves the following steps:

1. Set a purpose for searching.
2. Employ effective search strategies.
3. Analyze search-engine results.
4. Read critically and synthesize information.
5. Cite your sources.
6. How successful was your search? (p. 618)

Set a purpose for searching. The first and most crucial step is for students to have a clear goal or question in mind to focus their search. Prior to the search, allow students to spend time exploring a topic before choosing. Jumping right into identifying a question leads to low level learning and haphazard searching. For example, if a student is interested in researching horses, a typical search would result in over 174,000,000 sites. Teachers can help students with this step by asking them to think deeply about what information they are trying to locate. Consider the following questions:

1. What am I trying to find out about my topic? What do I want to know or solve?
2. What key words could I use in my search query?
3. Which of these key words are common or general words and which are more specific and would narrow the search?
4. What kind of information am I looking for? A definition, a description, a timeline, an image, a video or something else?

An IRT lesson in which the teacher models this process and then engages students in collaborative and independent practice with the process is important. Also, consider allowing students to use a printed or digital graphic organizer (see below for some suggestions) that will help them brainstorm in order to define and refine their topic and search terms.

Employ effective search strategies. Setting up an effective search for students involves several considerations. The first consideration is selecting how the data will be displayed. *How* information is displayed can be just as important as *what* information is displayed. For example, a search can be displayed linearly, which is the result of a traditional search, or visually through images, graphs, or timelines. InstaGrok (www. instagrok.com) is a search engine that presents search results in a graph (see Figure 8.1). Students can click on any of the key concepts to investigate in more depth. In addition, the right side of the screen displays key facts related to the topic, websites, videos, images, and quiz topic questions. Students can pin any of these representations to the graph. Another added feature of instaGrok is that a journal is automatically generated and saved, thereby documenting the students' search decisions as they annotate the graph. Teachers can create student accounts (without email addresses) and view the students' journals.

A second consideration is how to deal with unfiltered search results. Google is the most popular search engine used across platforms. However, a common concern among educators is the unfiltered results of any search that may result in the display of inappropriate content for students. To this end, teachers can create a customized search engine with Google Custom Search Engine (www.google.com/cse). Simply set up a Google educator account, choose the websites and resources you would like students to access, and follow the steps to create the search engine.

Gooru (www.goorulearning.org) searches only known, credible websites related to the user's query and allows users to refine their searches by content area, categories (e.g., slideshow, video, website), grade range or to search for a specific standard. Teachers can conduct a search on specific topics and organize their findings, into "collections" for their students to explore. Teachers can also include instructions or focus questions that will appear at the top of each page.

A third consideration for effective searches is the readability of the websites listed in the search results. With Google Custom Search Engine, teachers can also customize search results according to basic, intermediate, or advanced reading levels, which is

Figure 8.1. Instagrok Search Results for the Topic of Rainbows

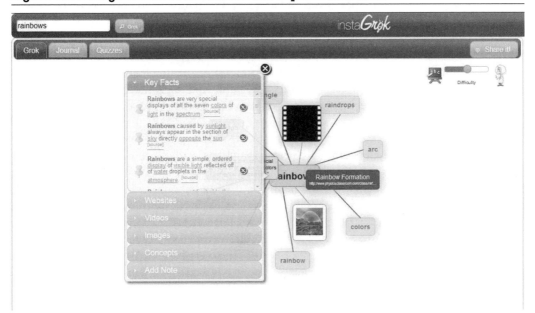

especially helpful for struggling readers. InstaGrok also allows users to adjust the difficulty level of the information presented via a slide bar at the top of the screen.

A fourth consideration for effective searches is the use of keywords. Knowing how to use Boolean search terms such as: and, or, not, +, –: and quotation marks can considerably narrow search results and increase the likelihood of finding useful information. For example, typing "civil war" + battles site:edu will ensure that the search engine will look for the term "civil war" rather than "civil" and "war"; the + will insure that these sites include battles, and site:edu will insure that the results will only come from education websites. For a tutorial on Boolean search terms go to: www.internettutorials.net.

Read critically. Once the search results have been displayed, students must then determine which results will provide the most relevant information to the search goal. It is helpful to be aware of research on how users search for information. Eye tracking research (Nielsen, 2006) has demonstrated that users read web content in an F-shaped pattern. The F-shape reading pattern refers to the viewing order: Users start by reading across the top line and then look down the page a little and read across again and then continue down the left side creating an F-shaped pattern. Thus, when reading search results, readers tend to skip wide sections of text as they search for relevant content. Quickly skimming and scanning search results is necessary since it would be unproductive to read every word. When students select a webpage, they should also skim the page for the URL, make inferences, and look for highlighted terms to determine if the information is relevant.

Additionally, students must learn to evaluate the content for authenticity, reliability, and reputability. Teachers can provide students with guidelines for what to look for when reading a website: identify the author or institution associated with the website, the purpose for the website, the intended audience, the appropriate copyright data, and whether the information meets the needs of the intended audience. More information on website evaluation is available at www.schrockguide.net/critical-evaluation.html.

After students have determined that a webpage is relevant and a credible source, teachers must teach them to move from skimming and scanning to reading closely. As discussed in Chapter 2, early immersion in online reading tends to reward multitasking and habituates the learner to immediate information gathering and quick attention shifts rather than deep reflection. Teachers can model effective online reading strategies, such as those described in Chapter 6, that will assist students in monitoring their reading habits so they adapt them to varying purposes and contexts.

There are several annotation tools that allow students to highlight and comment on material they are reading, viewing, or listening to that can assist students with close reading (see Table 8.1). The use of any or all of these tools assists students with monitoring their reading practices by providing an opportunity to annotate multiple forms of media, deepening the quality of analysis. Furthermore, all these tools are collaborative so students can work and learn from one another, and teachers can assess and scaffold when needed.

Synthesize information. Once students have gathered the information for their inquiry project, they will then need to organize and synthesize the information across

Table 8.1. Examples of Annotation Tools

Annotation Tool	Features That Support Close Reading
Diigo (www.diigo.com, see Figure 8.2) Webnotes (www.webnotes.net)	Both tools allow users to highlight, annotate, save, and share information on websites and PDF documents. Students and teachers can easily return to any bookmarked page and see their highlights and comments or extract annotations to include in a different document.
Markup (www.markup.io) Bounce (www.bounceapp.com)	Both tools allow users to draw or write on any webpage and then share their work with others. Regardless of how information is presented online (e.g., text, images, graphs) the ability to draw allows the user to make connections that otherwise would be difficult to make in another way.
VideoANT (ant.umn.edu) EmbedPlus (www.embedplus.com) Video Notes (www.videonotes)	These tools allow users to stream videos from YouTube and to crop, slow down, and add their own timed annotations to any video. Users can add external links, captions, calls-to-action, and comments during playback, and then embed final videos to multiple media sites such as websites, blogs, and wikis.
Thinglink (www.thinglink.com)	Allows users to upload images from a hard drive or import them from the web, Flickr, or Facebook, and then embed comments and links to other websites, music, photos, videos, or podcasts.

Note: All applications work on tablet or computer platforms.

multiple sources. There are several tools students can use to organize information. If students are conducting a search within Google Docs or using instaGrok, their search results have already been saved. Another way to collect and organize information is for students to add their sources to Evernote or Pinterest, as discussed in Chapter 7. Each of these tools allows students to see all of their sources in one place, review their annotations, and start sifting, selecting, and synthesizing the information.

Once students have decided on the information that is most meaningful to their inquiry, it is important that they synthesize it. How does the information from a webpage, a YouTube video, and images come together in a way that not only conveys the topic or concept of the inquiry but creates a new way of understanding? Thinking maps can be a helpful tool for displaying and categorizing information in ways that reveal new insights. Thinking maps visually represent patterns of thinking as mental models. Hyerle and Alper (2013) assert that thinking maps symbolically represent, define, and activate eight specific, interdependent cognitive processes as visual-verbal-spatial patterns:

- defining in context (labeling, definition)
- describing qualities (properties, characteristics, attributes)
- comparing and contrasting (similarities, differences)
- classification (classification, categorization, grouping)

- whole/part (spatial reasoning, physical structures)
- sequencing (ordering, seriation, cycles)
- cause–effect (causality, prediction, systems feedback)
- analogies (analogy, simile, metaphor, allegory) (pp. 108–109)

These interdependent mental operations require creative, interpretive, and reflective thinking.

InstaGrok provides a built-in thinking map, but several other mapping tools are available. Popplet (www.popplet.com), Coggle (www.coggle.it) and Text2Mindmap (www.text2mindmap.com) are three easy to use tools for displaying and categorizing information. Findery (www.findery.com) and Mapstory (www.mapstory.org) allow users to organize and display information in world, country, regional, or state maps, whereas Dipity (www.dipity.com) displays information on a timeline. These tools allow students to visualize information differently, thus revealing new insights and ideas that result in the creation of new information.

Cite your sources. It is important for students to understand that documentation of sources used from the Internet is a necessary part of any research. Citation is important because it allows people to acknowledge sources of information that are already known,

Figure 8.2. Annotated Webpage Using the Social Bookmarking Site Diigo

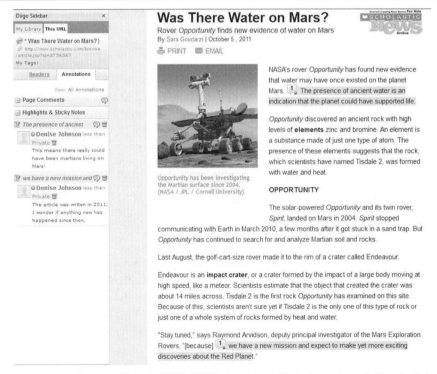

Source: From SCHOLASTIC NEWS, October 5, 2011. Copyright © 2011 by Scholastic Inc. Reprinted with permission of Scholastic Inc.

established, or thought as a basis for creating new knowledge. Using existing sources of information without acknowledgment is plagiarism, which is considered a serious offense. Teachers should make sure students understand the reason for citation as well as how to cite different sources such as websites, blogs, YouTube videos, and podcasts.

   EasyBib (www.easybib.com) is a free, easy to use citation service that can assist students in the format of source citations. InstaGrok automatically cites and saves sources. Google Docs (docs.google.com) also provides an easy way for students to conduct a search and cite sources. Google Docs allows users to create documents online that can be shared with others. In this way, several students researching the same document can collaborate. To conduct a search within Google Docs, follow the directions in Figure 8.3. The search results will open in a window to the right of the document. Students can see a preview of all search results without leaving the document. After selecting a site to include, a citation or a link will be placed in the document. In this way, the search results are organized and cited all in one place.

Figure 8.3. Search within Google Docs

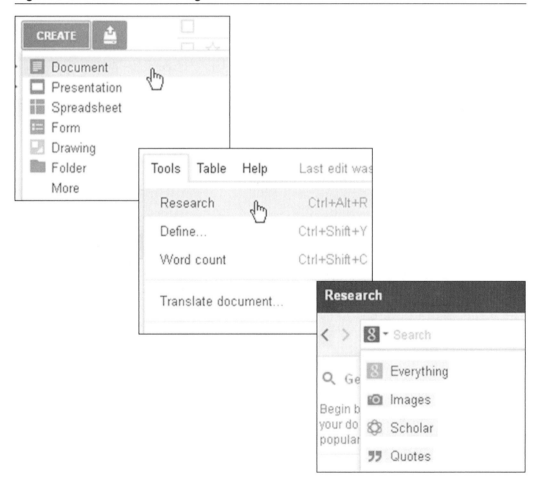

How successful was your search? Finally, students should reflect on the search process to identify the strategies they employed that were successful or unsuccessful and how they would change or refine their search strategies in the future. For example, did the selection of initial search terms provide search results with information specific to your topic or question? If not, how will you select search terms differently? Did your search results lead to credible and accurate information on your topic or question? If not, how will you define or refine your search differently? This is where the journal feature in instaGrok, the citation feature in Google Docs, or a simple traditional log used by students comes in handy.

Sharing New Information

Delivering well-crafted and executed presentations is a vital skill. Effective presentations involve multiple steps. Up to this point, students have spent a significant amount of time finding, reading, collecting, organizing, and synthesizing information on their topic of inquiry, but they must learn to convey that information in a concise and meaningful manner to their audience. Content, organization, delivery, and language are important aspects of effective presentations. Showing students examples of effective presentations is a good way to bring these elements to their attention and provide models.

The mode of presentation is also an important consideration. Table 8.2 provides an overview of a few software and online presentation programs.

In addition to these programs, Glogster (www.glogster.com) allows users to create Glogs, or interactive posters, that support text, graphics, music, videos, and can be shared on multiple platforms.

IRT FOR YOUNGER STUDENTS: ASKING WONDER QUESTIONS

Phase 1: Teacher modeling

Step 1: Planning the lesson. You will need a prepared example of how real-world text can lead to inquiry about your community and surroundings. If possible, take your class on a trip in the neighborhood or around the school to collect real-world reading/environmental print and take pictures. If this isn't possible, take several pictures of the school or community in advance.

A curriculum built on the foundation of engagement with content through questioning and critical thinking should begin as soon as young children walk through the school doors. For example, you can use children's immediate personal experiences to have them reflect on their own communities and how they use and think about the physical and built environment, which is a common science and/or social studies curriculum topic.

As mentioned in Chapter 4, the average entering kindergartner has a vocabulary of approximately 3,000 to 3,500 words. Since birth, these children have been acquiring an understanding of the sounds, words, grammar, and socially influenced meanings of the language they speak. Most of these words come from the language that is used in their homes and communities. They also learn to "read" many types of real-world texts. Children learn the importance of these types of text and even how to read some before they come to school. For example, while riding in the car, a child might see the "golden arches" and immediately know it is McDonalds. Children of all ages and reading abilities read and experience real-world text every day. As such, these texts are a great way to connect with and engage children to inquire into their home and school communities.

Step 2: Introduce the lesson. Tell students that, even though they are familiar with the people, places, and things in their everyday lives, they can learn even more about them if they ask wonder questions. Explain that scientists have made important discoveries based on questions that have arisen during their observations of everyday interactions. Note that authors also get writing ideas from these observations (see Figure 8.4). Inform students that, just like author Grace Lin, you are going to share wonder questions from your daily observations and then the students are going to think of their own wonder questions.

Step 3: Model the process. Share your wonder questions. Figure 8.5 is an example of my own wonder questions, which parallel the questions from Grace Lin's blog. Model the use of explicit language that scaffolds the link between observing and questioning, such as "When I look at the street signs in front of my house, I think about how strange they are and it makes me wonder . . ." or "When I look up at the full moon, I notice all of the white stuff around it and it makes me wonder. . . ." Ask students if they have any additional wonder questions based on your images.

Phase 2: Teacher and student demonstrations

Project an image taken around the school or community. Ask students to work in groups to brainstorm questions about the image.

Allow each group to share one of their questions. Then prompt students within each group to extend their thinking by reflecting on what sparked the question, such as "What made you wonder about. . . ."

Table 8.2. Presentation Software and Applications

Programs/Applications	Features
PowerPoint and Keynote software	Allows users to create audio, capture screenshots, and embed video. Finished presentations can be uploaded to YouTube or VoiceThread and shared online.
• VoiceThread (www.voicethread.com) • Animoto (www.animoto.com) • Google Presentation (docs.google.com) • Sliderocket (www.sliderocket.com) • Empressr (www.empressr.com) • Prezi (www.prezi.com)	These online presentation applications allow integration of audio, video, images, and text. Most of these applications allow finished presentations to be uploaded to YouTube or VoiceThread and shared online.

Figure 8.4. Everyday Observations from Grace Lin's Blog

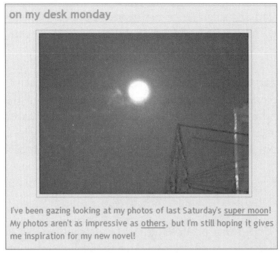

on my desk monday

I've been gazing looking at my photos of last Saturday's super moon! My photos aren't as impressive as others, but I'm still hoping it gives me inspiration for my new novel!

on the way to the grocery store

You just have to stop on Wigglesworth!

Source: www.gracelinblog.com/2010/08/on-way-to-grocery-store.html; www.gracelinblog.com/2011/03/on-my-desk-monday_21.html

After all groups have shared, ask if anyone thought of a new question after hearing all of the previous questions. Point out that sharing thinking often sparks new thinking.

Phase 3: Independent practice

Ask students to select a picture taken from a field trip or from home, and think of questions they may have about the picture. If no pictures are available, allow students to select a picture from your collection. When students have finished brainstorming questions, ask them to share their pictures and questions in groups of two or three. Then ask

Figure 8.5. Teacher Wonder Questions for 1st-Grade Community Study

The names of the streets near my
house are weird.
I wonder where the names come
from?

The full moon is so beautiful! I
wonder what
the white stuff is surrounding the
moon?

several students to share with the whole class. Ask students if they have new questions after discussing the pictures and questions with their groups.

Follow-up activity:

Figure 8.6 shows the culminating project of a 1st-grade science unit on understanding the life process of animals including their needs, physical characteristics, habitats, and adaptations. Each student in the class chose one of his or her questions and read numerous resources to find the answer to the questions. Often, the search for information led to new questions, curiosities, and interests. The students organized and displayed their questions, photos, and responses in a PowerPoint presentation that the entire class viewed together. The PowerPoint was also posted on the class website for parents to view. This activity can also be tied to the Wonder of the Day activity described in Chapter 4.

IRT LESSON FOR OLDER STUDENTS: DIGGING DEEP INTO INQUIRY

Phase 1: Teacher modeling

Step 1: Planning the lesson. You will need to decide which content area to teach and which presentation software to use. You also will need to create a paper or digital anchor chart, provide an F/Q/R response example (see below), and supply sticky notes for students

This IRT lesson will assist older students with understanding the importance of questioning when reading within any content area and delving deep into those

Figure 8.6. PowerPoint Presentation of 1st-Grade Students' Wonder Questions and Answers

questions to discover their true curiosities. Selecting an inquiry topic too quickly leads to superficial learning. To find questions that truly intrigue and sustain curiosity requires exploration.

This lesson will employ an F/Q/R anchor chart (Harvey, 1998), which includes Facts (expertise), Questions (critical thinking), and Response (motivation and engagement). The first column focuses on facts from the text that students find interesting. The second column allows students to ask questions based on the fact listed in the first column or a question derived from that fact. The third and final column is for personal response. This allows students to make connections, integrate their background knowledge of the topic, and synthesize this prior knowledge and new information. The structure of the F/Q/R chart encourages students to acknowledge their confusion while connecting details of a text to infer. Use it to ignite thinking about text-based questions and empower students to start and sustain new lines of inquiry. The chart also provides differentiated levels of support for ongoing practice.

Teachers can create the chart on paper (see Figure 8.7) or electronically. Padlet (padlet.com) is a simple application that allows users to post sticky notes to a virtual "wall." Each child in the class can add a note from a computer at the same time. A different wall can be created for facts, questions, and responses, and the walls can be saved as digital anchor charts or embedded in websites, blogs, or other media sites.

Step 2: Introduce the lesson. Display the sample F/Q/R anchor chart. Tell students you are going to model the process of your reading of nonfiction by thinking aloud about the facts presented in the text, the questions you have or things you wonder about those facts or the topic, and your response to the facts.

Step 3: Model the process. Read aloud a paragraph or section from a content-area textbook or nonfiction resource. Think aloud about your process of finding a fact in the section. Model writing or typing your fact on the anchor chart.

Ask a question or wonder about something related to the fact or topic. Write or type your question on the anchor chart.

Make a personal response based on your background knowledge of the fact and the connection to your question. Model writing or typing your response on the anchor chart.

Briefly review the processes involved in reading for text-based facts, asking questions or wondering about the fact or topic, and responding based on background knowledge and the connections to questions.

Phase 2: Teacher and student demonstrations

Divide students into groups of three. Give each group three sticky notes or access to the online space. Ask students to individually read the next section of the text and then, as a group, decide on one fact they find interesting and write it on one of the sticky notes.

Ask one student from each group to share the fact he or she wrote down and then either add the sticky note to the chart or type the fact on the digital chart.

Figure 8.7. F/Q/R Chart Created by 4th-Graders

Facts	Questions	Response

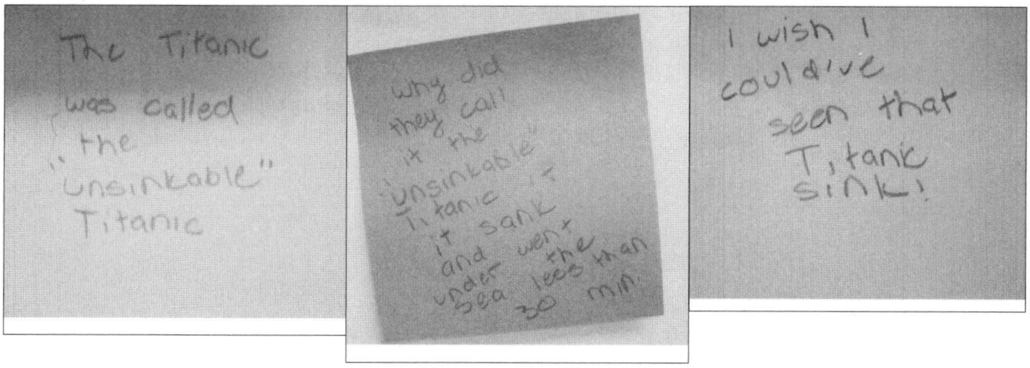

After each group shares a fact, scaffold the students' thinking about questions they might ask about that fact. Ask each group to write down one question on a second sticky note.

Ask one student from each group to share the question and then either add the sticky note to the chart or type the question on the digital chart.

Ask students to think about the fact and question they have generated in their groups. Ask them to think about what they already know about the topic and make connections to their question to come up with a personal response. Then ask one student from each group to share the response and either add the sticky note to the chart or type the response on the digital chart.

Discuss the unique questions and connections different groups made based on their individual experiences and interests. This collaboration is what makes learning fun!

Phase 3: Independent practice

Give students the opportunity to continue reading on their own. Students can continue to write facts, questions, and responses on sticky notes to add to the class chart or they can write them in a reading response journal or online writing space such as a blog or wiki. Be sure to bring students back together as a group to share their facts, questions, and responses.

Follow-up activity:

Allow students to gather facts, questions, and responses within a content-area topic over the course of a unit. Then, take their curiosity a step further, and allow them to focus on one of their questions to dig deeper into inquiry. Providing students with more time to explore a topic before choosing helps them choose something worthy of inquiry (see Figure 8.8). As noted, jumping right into identifying a question can lead to low-level learning.

Figure 8.8. Dear Reader Letter from 4th-Grader about His Research Project

Dear Reader,

My name is Anthony and I was going to research all of the creatures of the ocean. My teacher said that you should do a topic that you are very interested in so I said the whole sea. But I said maybe I should narrow it down to one creature. And I found that doing all of them was hard. And so I had to do one subject. I had a hard time choosing a creature out of all of them! It was hard. But one stood out a lot. The Dumbo Octopus! It was a weird topic. But weird was interesting. Very interesting. And cute.

Your writer: Anthony

CHAPTER 9

Assessment in a Literacy 2.0 Environment

A critical issue for learning is the extent to which assessments focus on valuable content and generative skills that enable transfer of what is learned to new problems and settings, rather than focusing on lower level skills of recall and recognition alone. Also, teachers' abilities to learn from the assessment information make a difference for whether results translate into more productive teaching or simply result in failure and stigma for struggling students.

—Linda Darling-Hammond, *The Flat World and Education* (2010, p. 7)

The technology applications discussed in Chapters 3 through 8 have the ability to engage students in authentic, creative, and collaborative learning in which students use both traditional and new literacies for meaningful knowledge construction. It is important that teachers have meaningful assessments that capture both the process and products of new literacies.

Assessment *for* instruction—the process of seeking and interpreting evidence to decide where the learners are in their learning, where they need to go, and how best to get there—is important in digital environments, and requires that students demonstrate *what* they know, and explain *why* they know it. Assessments that capture evidence of learning new literacies largely don't exist; therefore, teachers may need to adapt familiar tools or create new forms of assessment to correspond to these learning opportunities.

NCTE's 21st Century Literacies Framework (2008), discussed in Chapter 2, includes implications of the framework for assessments. Following the same question format as the framework, Figure 9.1 includes both traditional purposes for assessment and the possible components and elements of assessment that may be new for 21st-century student work.

From this list, assessments must capture students' understanding of how to use technology tools, their dispositions toward the use of technology tools, and their ability to use new literacies to read, write, listen, view, and communicate effectively with these tools. With this in mind, a review of research (Coiro, 2009) reveals that effective assessments of new literacies should:

- be paired with instruction, learner-centered, ongoing, and authentic
- support students' self-reflection and self-regulation of skills and strategies
- engage students in self, peer, and teacher reviews of their online reading strategies
- include multiple assessments and alternative forms of assessment
- evaluate online learning products and processes

Figure 9.1. Traditional and New Elements of Assessment of 21st-Century Student Learning

Traditional elements of assessment of 21st-century student learning

- Do students use sources of information that are relevant and reliable in developing the product?
- What is the significance of new information or understandings conveyed in the final product?
- Is the product effective in achieving its purpose and on impacting the audience?
- Do students demonstrate creativity, initiative, and effectiveness in the process of solving problems and in the final product?
- Do students use legal and ethical processes and behaviors?

New elements of assessment of 21st-century student learning

- Do students have access to 21st-century tools in and out of school?
- Do students have access to a range in the depth and breadth of information?
- Do students have the capacity to use technology tools?
- Can tools in the arts and design be used by students not traditionally trained in those fields?
- Can students use images and sound to amplify text?
- Can students create products that emulate those of professionals?
- Do students receive feedback from experts in the field?
- Do students interact with and have an impact on a global audience?
- Can students select tools or media that most effectively communicate the intention of the product?
- Do students engage in the use of ethical and legal practice as they remix products?
- Do students engage in ethical and safe online behavior?

Adapted from the NCTE (2008) *NCTE Framework for 21st-Century Curriculum and Assessment.*

Additionally, a critical aspect of classroom assessment is to engage students deeply in the process and increase the specific, descriptive feedback they receive while they are learning. For example, teachers can create an assessment that defines expectations for assignments or activities, such as a rubric for writing blogs discussed in Chapter 7. With teacher instruction, demonstration, and ongoing support, students can use the assessment as a guideline for completing assignments. Teachers can meet with students individually to provide feedback as to whether they are meeting the expectations outlined on the assessment. In this way, assessments allow students to take responsibility for their learning while informing the teacher's instruction for meeting students' needs.

ASSESSMENT TOOLS

Assessment is often viewed in terms of formative and summative. Formative assessment, or assessment *for* learning, focuses on the process of learning, is ongoing, and provides information needed to adjust teaching and support learning. Formative assessment helps teachers monitor students' processing and understanding of an activity such as reading a webpage or writing a blog post, and assists with gauging student readiness to proceed to further tasks. Summative assessment, or assessment *of* learning, focuses on learning at a particular point, such as a cumulative project or activity at the end of a unit, and provides information on the learning outcomes. Both assessments are valuable; however, formative assessments are most important in assisting students with acquiring the skills and strategies of new literacies and informing instruction.

The following sections describe a variety of assessment tools that teachers can use to capture students' thinking processes and products as they use new literacies. Existing assessments can be repurposed along with the new tools of technology for capturing students' skills, strategies, and dispositions of new literacies.

Observation and Feedback

Observation, or kid watching, is one of the most powerful assessment tools. As teachers observe a student engaged in a particular activity, they note if he or she does the following:

- performs the activity proficiently
- uses appropriate skills, strategies, and dispositions
- progresses in knowledge of appropriate skills, strategies, and dispositions
- performs or produces a product adequately

Be sure to find a system for recording and organizing observations that enables you to remember and use the information to inform instruction. Observational or anecdotal notes can be recorded in numerous ways, such as the following:

- audio or video recordings of students explaining their thinking about a text or process, or performing a skill, strategy, or activity. Teachers can include typed or recorded observations on the recording.
- photos of student work with typed or recorded observations
- screen shots of Web 2.0 work with typed or recorded observations
- individual conferencing notes typed directly into a document and saved to a folder for each child. (See Figure 9.2 for an Evernote example.)

Most often, anecdotal notes are for reference only and not shared with students. However, students need direct feedback on their use of new literacies to know if they are meeting expectations and to aid their continual growth. In addition to face-to-face conversations with students, teachers can share feedback through audio recordings (e.g., VoiceThread), blog comments, and virtual sticky notes (e.g., Diigo and Webnotes).

Another important form of feedback can be acquired directly from students. A long-standing form of feedback has been students' responses to teacher-generated questions or from students raising their hands to ask questions. Obvious drawbacks are that shy or unsure students may not raise their hands. Several technology tools can help give all students an opportunity to respond:

Figure 9.2. Cathy Mere's Evernote Notebook for Collecting Student Assessment Information

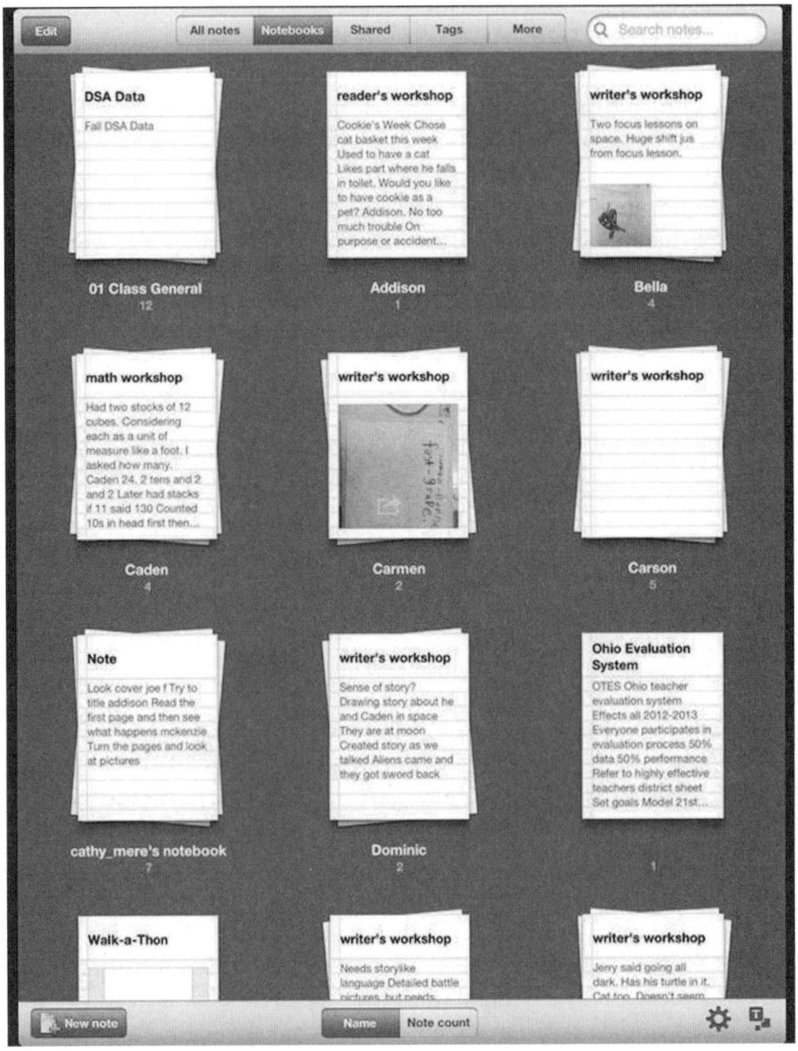

Source: www.reflectandrefine.blogspot.com/2012/09/six-ways-to-use-evernote-to-capture.html

- Backchanneling provides a virtual room in which students type questions or comments in real-time while the teacher is providing instruction. TodaysMeet (www.todaysmeet.com) and Google Moderator (www.google.com/moderator) are easy-to-use sites that host backchanneling.
- Instant messaging is similar to backchanneling. A good site for hosting chat sessions is Chatzy (www.chatzy.com).
- Twitter enables students to add a common hashtag the teacher creates to their tweets to make comments.
- Live blogging allows students to post questions and comments on their blog.

Be sure to look at questions and comments throughout instruction to know if students understand. Then provide individual feedback or address comments and questions in subsequent lessons.

Inventories and Surveys

Merriam-Webster's online dictionary defines an inventory as "an itemized list of current assets" (n.d.). This is a great way to think about the use of inventories and surveys in the classroom to provide an itemized list of each child's current assets! Attitude and interest inventories have long been used as a way to ascertain whether students like to read and what they like to read. Similarly, inventories are a good way to get an overall picture of students' attitudes toward and proficiency with technology. Items on an inventory, or survey, can be read aloud to very small children, and students' responses can take the form of emoticons, smiley or frowny faces, that are circled. Surveymonkey.com is a great, easy-to-use application for quickly creating online surveys.

Checklists

Checklists provide a structured list of observable characteristics relative to the task, skill, or strategy that serve as a frame of reference to guide observations. Checklists enable a teacher to become more knowledgeable about a student's strengths and needs in a particular area. Use checklists such as the one in Table 9.1 as a benchmark at the beginning, middle, and end of the year to record progress over time.

Rubrics

Rubrics, which have been discussed in previous chapters, are performance-based scoring guides to assess and evaluate the quality of a student's work against a predetermined set of criteria. They also articulate gradations of quality for each criterion, from excellent to poor. Therefore, rubrics focus on an expected learning outcome while representing a broad range of abilities and serving as a guide for learning. Rubrics can be powerful tools for both instruction and assessment; they "improve student performance as well as monitor it by making teachers' expectations clear and by showing students how to meet these expectations" (Goodrich, 1997, p. 14). The design of a rubric is critical to its effectiveness.

For rubrics to be most effective, teachers should engage students in their creation. Goodrich (1997) recommends the following guidelines:

1. *Look at models:* Show students examples of good and not-so-good work. Identify the characteristics that make the good ones good and the bad ones bad.
2. *List criteria:* Use the discussion of models to begin a list of what counts in quality work.
3. *Articulate gradations of quality:* Describe the best and worst levels of quality, then fill in the middle levels based on your knowledge of common problems and the discussion of not-so-good work.

4. *Practice on models:* Have students use the rubrics to evaluate the models you gave them in Step 1.
5. *Use self- and peer-assessment:* Give students their task. As they work, stop them occasionally for self- and peer-assessment.
6. *Revise:* Always give students time to revise their work based on the feedback they get in Step 5.
7. *Use teacher assessment:* Use the same rubric students used to assess their work yourself. (pp. 15–16)

Rubrics present a continuum of performance that allows teachers to identify similar performances from students in their classroom to see how far or close to standard they are. Noted educator Kathy Schrock has many examples of rubrics for Web 2.0 tools and learning at www.schrockguide.net/assessment-and-rubrics.html. RubiStar (rubistar.4teachers.org) allows users to build their own rubric.

Portfolios

Ultimately, the measure of a successful school year stems from looking at a student's work. Yet, as is common across the United States, students often throw away their work sent home from school. Consider the following excerpt from a blog post written by educator and digital learning consultant Wesley Fryer (2010):

> [Y]esterday I watched my 11 year old son "throw away sixth grade" into our trash can outside. There was a LOT of important learning which went into that trash can, and is now somewhere in an Oklahoma City dump. I wish more of those learning artifacts were online so we could see them as parents, and he could have them as part of his academic digital footprint.

Fryer's words are very thought provoking. Schools and students can benefit immensely from collecting and reflecting on student work over time, and storing that work in a digital portfolio prevents the situation in the blog post from happening.

A digital portfolio is a multimedia collection of student work:

> When done well . . . a digital portfolio outlines a student's learning journey in much the same way that a curriculum map describes a teacher's teaching journey. The collection of

Table 9.1. Checklist for Observing Technology Dispositions

Observable Indicators	Often	Sometimes	Not Yet

work in a portfolio can do two things: it can show that a student has met standards and show who the student is as an individual learner. (Niguidula, 2010, p. 154)

Teachers and students should work together to determine what student work will be collected in the portfolio. It is important that the platform used to house a student's portfolio allows incorporation of multiple media; is easy to use, organize, and customize; and stays in the cloud so students have access outside of school. Blogs, VoiceThread, Evernote, wikis, and Google sites are ideal platforms.

The heart of a portfolio is reflection. Feedback from teachers, peers, and outside experts should be included, along with the student's self-reflection on the artifacts. Students can write or record reflections on what they learned from completing projects or how their learning has developed over time. For example, a student could compare his or her digital storytelling project (see Chapter 3) completed at the beginning of the year with another project completed toward the end of the year, reflecting on how the combination of images, music, and text to convey his or her message has changed over time. Portfolio reflection must be structured and intentional—otherwise it becomes an electronic file cabinet. Helen Barrett, known as the grandmother of electronic portfolios, offers additional information on electronic portfolios on her website at www.electronicportfolios.org.

ASSESSING NEW LITERACIES

The forms of assessment described in the previous sections can be used in myriad ways to engage students in demonstrating how they can read, write, communicate, and organize information to solve problems, frame and conduct inquiries, analyze and synthesize data, and apply learning to new situations. The following sections discuss how to use assessments to capture students' technology skills and dispositions, online reading comprehension and composition processes, and culminating multimedia projects.

Technology Skills and Dispositions

With the prevalence of technology in today's society, even very young children come to school with technology skills and dispositions toward the use of technology. Many families have an electronic reading device (Kindle, Nook), iPad, cell phone, digital camera, or computer at home, with which children have interacted from a very early age. Each device uses a specific vocabulary to describe its functions and tools (app, mouse) and requires unique navigation. Therefore, it may be helpful to conduct an assessment of students' technology skills and dispositions early in the school year. For example, create a simple survey that can be administered to the whole class and read out loud to young children or that older students can complete on the computer.

After introducing students to technology tools and strategies for using them, teachers should see a shift over time in students' ability to use them in more advanced and purposeful ways that reflect their knowledge of the content and audience. Therefore, teachers will want to build a component into their assessment for observing this shift. Table 9.2 is a rubric developed by Johnson (2011) for this purpose.

Table 9.2. Rubric for Assessing Students' Use of Technology when Creating Products

Category	4	3	2	1
Consideration of Audience	Strong awareness of audience in the design. Students can clearly explain how the choices they made fit the target audience.	Some awareness of audience in the design. Students can partially explain how the choices they made fit the target audience.	Students are able to describe the target audience and their needs, but project lacks evidence of this understanding.	Limited awareness of the needs and interests of the target audience. Cannot clearly identify their intended audience.
Justified Choices	Students are able to clearly link every design choice to content. Creativity is consistently shown in how the content ties into each choice.	Able to link most of the choices made to content. Can clearly describe decision-making process.	Able to link some of the choices made to content. Cannot clearly describe decisionmaking process.	Unable to justify any choices made.
Content Addressed Accurately	All facts are accurate.	90–99% of the facts are accurate.	80–89% of the facts are accurate.	Fewer than 80% of the facts are accurate.
Creativity Expressed	Product is easily identified as the creator's work. Can look at projects and know who created it without asking!	Creator of the product can be identified somewhat easily. Audience is able to tell something about the creator's personality.	Difficult to identify the creator of the product, but project is attractive and tells a little about the creator's personality.	Product shows little to no creativity. The project is dull and tells nothing of the creator's personality.

Source: Digital tools for teaching © 2011 by Capstone. All rights reserved.

Dispositions are the attitudes or tendencies students bring to any activity involving new literacies. These dispositions will continually develop as students engage in more and different experiences with technology. Leu, Leu, and Coiro (2004) identified the following important dispositions of new literacies:

- Posing a "problem definition disposition," recognizing that Internet resources are often helpful to better understand a problem. As you gather background information about the general nature of the issues involved, the Internet helps you ask the right questions.
- Having a "multiple search strategy disposition," considering multiple search strategy possibilities, and quickly evaluating the potential of each one for a given purpose.

- Having a "healthy skeptic disposition," always evaluating each piece of information that you encounter, thinking critically about information found on the Internet.
- Having a "nonlinear disposition," seeking out multiple types and sources of information and continually thinking across texts and other media about their meaning.
- Having a "communication disposition," knowing that communication with a large number of people can have an important impact if done successfully, efficiently, and ethically. (pp. 23–24)

These dispositions lead to the readers' ability to display persistence, flexibility, collaboration, critical stance, and reflection when reading challenging online texts. It is important to be aware of where students are in developing these dispositions. Observing individual students as they engage in online activities presents opportunities to assess the development of these dispositions within the context of specific activities. A simple checklist (see Table 9.1) will provide feedback on the development of these dispositions over time. A formal survey that is to be administered to students (Table 9.3) will provide more in-depth information.

Collaboration is another important disposition. As stated in NCTE's 21st Century Literacies Framework (2008), twenty-first century readers and writers need to build relationships with others to pose and solve problems collaboratively and cross-culturally. Ways to engage students in collaborative activities have been described throughout the chapters in this book. Teachers will need to create new assessments that capture students' interpersonal communication skills, ability to effectively engage in team work, appreciation of differences in cultural practices and work patterns, and the ability to respond appropriately to peer feedback (Coiro, 2009). Table 9.4 provides a collaboration rubric created by Johnson (2011).

Online Reading Comprehension and Composition

The new generation of assessments for the Common Core State Standards will be conducted completely online and require students to respond to multiple-choice items (some of which are technology-enhanced), open-ended responses, and performance assessments. Performance tasks involve writing after getting information from multiple sources. This information might come from two or more texts, video or audio clips, or visuals and the information gained from these sources is then used in a writing activity. An example from a 4th-grade performance task asks students to read an article and watch a video about how animals defend themselves from danger and then write an article about an animal described in the sources for the purpose of inclusion in a museum display on animal defenses.

The implications for instruction of the item types mean that students will need strategies for effective online reading comprehension and composition. These processes include prior knowledge of website structures, inferential reasoning strategies, and self-regulated reading processes, and integrating and synthesizing multiple media sources of information as well as an understanding of navigation.

Table 9.3. Survey of Online Reading Dispositions

	Strongly disagree	Disagree	Agree	Strongly agree
1. I believe it's very important for me to learn how to use the Internet.				
2. I would work harder if I could use the Internet more often in school.				
3. I believe the Internet makes it harder to get useful information.				
4. I can learn many things when I use the Internet.				
5. I think kids who don't use the Internet miss out on a lot of important information.				

Open-Ended Questions

What is easiest for you about using the Internet for research?

What is hardest for you about using the Internet for research?

Can you think of a time when you had trouble finding something using the Internet? How do you feel when this happens? How long do you keep trying before you give up?

What do you know about using the Internet effectively that some kids your age might not know?

What do you know about using the Internet effectively that some adults might not know?

Printed with permission from Julie Coiro (2009). Rethinking online reading assessment. *Educational Leadership, 66*(6), 59–63.

Observation is one of the best tools for assessing online reading comprehension. Many teachers hold one-on-one conferences with their students during which they ask students to read a selection from the text they are reading independently and then discuss their understanding of that selection and/or how it fits into their overall comprehension of the text. These individual conferences provide an opportunity to see the students' reading and comprehension processes in action and to provide immediate feedback. These conferences provide the same valuable information from online reading. Ask students to read a piece of online text and then describe the strategies they used when confronted with aspects of the text, such as embedded hyperlinks, videos, and images. It is easy to record digital conference notes or conference conversations as a student thinks aloud. Teachers can then analyze them at a later time and share them with parents. Table 9.5 presents a rubric for assessing students' strategies for reading a webpage, and Table 9.6 presents a survey for conducting a web search.

Several other digital sources, discussed in Chapters 3 through 8, also provide insight into students' online reading comprehension strategies:

- individual and collaborative digital writing projects and peer critiques (Chapters 3, 7, and 8)
- Kindle and Nook annotations and notes (Chapters 5 and 6)
- response to reading on blogs/comments on others' blogs (Chapter 7)
- Diigo/Webnotes annotations and notes (Chapter 8)
- Internet search via instaGrok or web search log (Chapter 8)

Teachers should also hold one-on-one writing conferences with their students to discuss each child's writing. As discussed in Chapter 7, writing involves the reciprocal process of reading, so assessment should include the process of understanding audience awareness; synthesizing, analyzing, and evaluating information; linking information;

Table 9.4. Collaboration Rubric

Category	4	3	2	1
Group Problem Solving	Actively looks for and suggests solutions to problems.	Refines solutions suggested by others.	Does not suggest or refine solutions, but is willing to try out solutions suggested by others.	Does not try to solve problems or help others solve problems. Lets others do the work.
Focus on the Task	Consistently stays focused on the task and what needs to be done. Very self-directed.	Focuses on the task and what needs to be done most of the time. Other group members can count on this person.	Focuses on the task and what needs to be done some of the time. Other group members must sometimes nag and prod to keep this person on-task.	Rarely focuses on the task and what needs to be done. Lets others do the work.
Mutual Respect	Actively seeks to incorporate other group members' opinions, ideas, or contributions.	Incorporates some of the other group members' opinions, ideas, or contributions into the project.	Recognizes the value of other group members' opinions, ideas, or contributions.	Puts down other group members' opinions, ideas, or contributions.
Value to Group	Routinely provides useful ideas when participating in the group and in classroom discussion. A definite leader who contributes a lot of effort.	Usually provides useful ideas when participating in the group and in classroom discussion. A strong group member who tries hard.	Sometimes provides useful ideas when participating in the group and in classroom discussion. A satisfactory group member who does what is required.	Rarely provides useful ideas when participating in the group and in classroom discussion. May refuse to participate.

Source: Digital tools for teaching © 2011 by Capstone. All rights reserved.

Table 9.5. Rubric for Assessing Strategies for Reading a Webpage

Strategy	Beginner	Developing	Proficient
Structure	Overwhelmed by webpage content—i.e., has a difficult time determining where to start reading/viewing/listening	Familiar with webpage structure but doesn't always use it to construct meaning	Familiar with webpage structure and uses it to construct meaning
Skimming and scanning web content	Uses inefficient strategies, such as reading content word for word, and/or is unsure of what to look for to determine relevance and reliability	Skims content but isn't always sure if information is relevant or reliable	Skims the webpage for key words to determine if information is relevant and reliable
Navigation	Unsure of how to navigate the webpage, randomly selects linked sources, often gets lost, and is unable to return to original source	Understands how to navigate the webpage but sometimes, when moving through several pages, is unsure how to return to the original source	Understands how to navigate and uses effective strategies for returning to the original source
Inferring hyperlinked text	Selects linked text without inferring whether the information behind the link will be relevant, helpful, or valid	Often infers relevance, usefulness, and validity of hyperlinked text before selecting	Always infers relevance, usefulness, and validity of hyperlinked text before selecting
Inferring media	Selects embedded audio/video without inferring whether the content will be relevant, useful, or valid	Often infers relevance, usefulness, and validity of media before selecting	Always infers relevance, usefulness, and validity of media before selecting
Using tools to figure out unknown words and build background knowledge	Doesn't use tools, such as an online dictionary, to figure out unknown words or use available resources, such as embedded audio/video, to build prior knowledge for understanding content	Often accesses tools to figure out unknown words and uses available resources to build prior knowledge for understanding content	Always accesses tools to figure out unknown words and uses available resources to build prior knowledge for understanding content

and choosing graphics or video to support writing. Observations, checklists, or rubrics can be created to assess one or more of these processes. For example, Table 9.2 presents a rubric for understanding audience awareness and selecting multimedia.

Projects

Multimedia projects are typically summative in that they are the culminating part of a larger series of tasks such as forming an inquiry, conducting a web search, reading,

Table 9.6. Think-Aloud Survey for Conducting an Internet Search

My name: _____   My partner's name: _____

Date of think-aloud sharing: _____ Topic of inquiry:

_____

I will check how I think my partner used think-alouds with me.	**I agree**	**I disagree**	**I'm not sure**
My partner told me **why** he or she picked the website based on the topic.			
My partner explained to me **how** he or she was browsing the website.			
My partner explained **why** he or she selected a main idea from the website to record on the graphic organizer.			
My partner explained to me **how** the main idea would be recorded on the graphic organizer.			
My partner told me **what** details about the main idea he or she selected from the website and **why** they were chosen.			
My partner explained **how** the details would be recorded on the graphic organizer.			
Check what you think about using think-alouds with your partner today.			
Today, the think-alouds helped me to know what goes on when someone reads information on the Internet.			

If you want to share anything more about today's think-aloud time, please write all about it below. Thanks!

analyzing, evaluating, and synthesizing search results, compiling results, and designing an effective presentation. Teachers may use a number of formative assessments for each aspect of the project and then a summative rubric to assess the final project (an example of a checklist for students appears in Figure 9.3).

ORGANIZING AND SHARING ASSESSMENT INFORMATION

How has assessment changed? Consider the following excerpt:

> Julie keeps a notebook with a divider for each child in the class. Each time she meets with a child individually or in a group, she places her sticky notes or observation sheets in the notebook with the appropriate child. Each day, she looks over the notes she has made in order to plan for the next day's instruction. Julie knows that keeping track of her students' literacy development is important to providing the appropriate support for continued progress. (Johnson, 2008, p. 93)

Today, assessment is just as important in Julie's 4th-grade classroom, but notebooks, dividers, sticky notes, and observation sheets are a thing of the past. Julie keeps the same information online for ease of access, plus she is able to include many more types of artifacts.

Cathy Mere, a 1st-grade teacher, has also moved away from keeping paper copies of ongoing assessment. After using a spiral notebook for 10 years, Cathy now uses Evernote to capture student learning and recording her conferences and notes (see Figure 9.2). She believes that the use of Evernote has caused her assessment to become much deeper and richer. Evernote can serve as a central space to house a vast collection of multimedia assessment data for each child—including audio recordings, snapshots, scanned work or images, webpages, written notes, video, and Google documents and forms—and supports a number of ways to organize and access information by tagging and sorting. Another application offering similar options is Three Ring (www.threering.com).

With one click, Evernote displays all the assessment data for one student or all students. This allows for analysis across multiple sources and types of data, providing a deeper, richer picture of student learning. It is also helpful for sharing with other teachers, school personnel such as reading specialists, and parents. Cathy Mere has written about her use of Evernote on her blog *Reflect and Refine* (www.reflectandrefine.blogspot.com). In response to one of Cathy's posts, teacher debf (2012) left the following comment:

> My newest love is emailing parents directly from EN [Evernote]!
> I have added all the parent email addresses to my contacts making emailing from EN seamless! In addition, I added a Parent Communication note for each child. This note contains all parent contact information and a family photo. I find having the photo handy helps me to remember my parent communications. I can email parents notes, photos, videos or audio clips as I sit alongside the child!
> The kids LOVE this, I even let the kids hit the "send" button.

Assessment is a critical aspect of teaching and learning. Using tools such as Evernote can make the process easier while extending the depth and complexity of analysis. It also makes it easier to share assessments with other stakeholders.

Figure 9.3. Checklist for Multimedia Projects

Preparation

- I planned my time wisely.
- I stated my plan for the project clearly.
- I made a list of materials I would need for the project.
- I knew what I had to find, make, or do before I began.

Resources

- I used newspapers or magazines to find information.
- I used books, encyclopedias, or textbooks to find information.
- I used the Internet or a CD-ROM to find information.
- I watched videos or television to find information.
- I looked at drawings or paintings to find information.
- I made a list of things I planned to use in my project.

Media

- I used my own art.
- I used photographs.
- I used voice, sound, or music.
- My media made my presentation more interesting.
- My media made my presentation clearer.
- My media does not distract the user.
- I made buttons that allow the user to turn the sound or music on and off.
- I made a list of the media made by others that I used in my presentation.

Organization

- I made an outline, idea map, or storyboard to organize my thoughts.
- I included a meaningful title.
- I included my name and the names of people in my group.
- My presentation explained my topic clearly.
- I organized my ideas so they made sense to others.
- I included interesting or exciting information.
- I used pictures or sounds to make the presentation more interesting.
- I included a strong ending to my presentation.
- I included a list of the things I used to find information.

Navigation

- Users can easily view the whole presentation.
- Users can easily skip parts of the presentation.
- Users can easily repeat or go back to part of the presentation.

Figure 9.3. Checklist for Multimedia Projects (continued)

- The buttons and links are easy to see.
- The buttons and links are in the same place on different cards/slides.
- The buttons and links work.
- The buttons and links are labeled.
- The cards/slides are titled so users can tell where they are.

Appearance

- The words on my slides are easy to read.
- The words on my slides are spelled correctly.
- Titles and headings are easy to read.
- The pictures on my slides are easy to see.
- The pictures are related to the information on the slides.
- The colors and patterns on my slides look good together.
- Sounds and music are easy to hear and understand.
- There is enough time to read/see/listen to everything on each slide.
- The transitions between slides are not distracting or boring.
- There is not too much or too little time between slides.

CHAPTER 10

What About Literacy 3.0?
Continuing Professional Development

Just as Literacy 1.0 become Literacy 2.0, when will Literacy 2.0 become Literacy 3.0? Coiro, Knobel, Lankshear, and Leu (2008) write:

> Given the increasingly rapid appearance of continuously new technologies of literacy on the Internet, this aspect of new literacies may become more important, in the long run, than even the speed with which access to the Internet is spreading around the world. It suggests that new literacies will continuously be new, multiple, and rapidly disseminated. (p. 5)

Teachers are often technology users, but staying abreast of the continuous development of technology that could impact literacy learning and the acquisition of new literacies takes considerable time and planning. Most teachers have had a college course and/or inservice training on using technology; however, effective classroom practice doesn't usually result from a course or one shot inservice. Effective professional development must be flexible, ongoing, job embedded, and meet teachers' specific needs with opportunities for coaching, reflection, and collaboration with colleagues (Darling-Hammond, Wei, Andree, Richardson, & Orphanos, 2009). Collaboration with colleagues has been found to significantly improve teaching quality (Jackson & Bruegmann, 2009; National Center for Literacy Education, 2013). However, this kind of professional development and time for collaboration are rare (MetLife Survey of American Teachers, 2013).

New models of professional development that circumvent many of the obstacles of traditional models are quickly becoming more prevalent. These models allow teachers to use digital tools and social networking to plan, collaborate, and learn from other educators in their schools, across the United States, and around the world. The benefits of "anywhere, anytime" online professional learning that provides teachers with instant access to a network of colleagues who have useful skills and knowledge have been documented by research (Reeves & Li, 2012).

PROFESSIONAL DEVELOPMENT NETWORKS

Networked learning can be a powerful way of creating sustained professional development driven by teacher needs. The best way to get started is by implementing networked learning models and discussing their use with other teachers considering similar in-structional decisions. Two models that foster networked professional development are professional learning communities (PLCs) and professional learning networks (PLNs).

Professional Learning Communities

Near the beginning of the school year, I met a colleague for lunch who is the assis-tant principal of a local elementary school. During our conversation, she excitedly told me that the schools in her district had started PLCs. She explained that each school had decided on a digital tool it wanted to investigate for improving student learning and engagement. Her school had chosen blogs. All the teachers and administrators in the school had Twitter accounts, which they used to communicate ideas for projects, lesson plans, and student work and participation, and to troubleshoot, share frustrations, and celebrate successes. She shared many exciting stories about the way blogs were being used throughout the school for meaningful learning. Some teachers were initially hesi-tant either because they were "digital immigrants" (Prensky, 2001) and worried about their technology skills, or because they were worried about the value of using blogs. By sharing their experiences and expertise with one another, however, they were able to provide the support needed to alleviate these concerns.

As you have probably already deduced, a PLC consists of all teachers and adminis-trators within a school working collectively and collaboratively on an inquiry through shared planning and curriculum development; accessing resources within and out-side the school; and providing feedback, support, or coaching for teachers. Successful implementation of a PLC requires extensive and sustained planning. Richardson and Mancabelli (2011) recommend a year-long pilot project in which select teachers and administrators who are committed to change and who already use technology use stra-tegically chosen digital tools to achieve key learning goals. They share reflections on the use of these tools, how teachers can collaboratively plan to use them, and ways to provide technical support.

A critical component of PLCs is communication. It is essential for teachers to plan, reflect, and problem solve in ways that support ongoing inquiry and integration; how-ever, time to meet face to face is limited. My friend's school used Twitter for this pur-pose, but there are many other alternatives, including the creation of an online space for collecting and housing shared documents and supporting ongoing communication of ideas and inquiries that will be discussed later in this chapter.

Near the end of the school year, I had the opportunity to meet my friend again for lunch. She reflected on how many teachers in her school had started to blog about their teaching and connected with educators at other schools in the district and around the world. Communicating with others had broadened their access to expertise and their interest in other digital tools. Several teachers were engaging their students in the use of additional digital tools and online activities due to the influence of their own PLN.

Professional Learning Networks

Online tools can help teachers find and connect with colleagues and capitalize on a variety of virtual professional learning opportunities. Teachers build these online PLNs by subscribing to professional learning sites to acquire and share ideas and resources. The different types of PLNs and tools available and examples of each type are in Figure 10.1.

Managing information. The amount of information available through the PLNs and related tools listed in Figure 10.1 can be overwhelming. In fact, visiting all these sources daily is impossible. Teacher-librarian, John Schu (2013), who is also a blogger, notes, "I spend too much time tweeting, blogging, emailing, reading status updates, bouncing from blog to blog, and getting lost in the Internet." A Really Simple Syndication (RSS) reader can help by aggregating multiple sources of information. RSS readers use RSS feeds to collect new posts, articles, and updates from websites identified by the user, and deliver this information to the RSS Reader (see Figure 10.2). In this way, teachers can quickly skim through and read the information of interest when they have time. Examples of RSS readers include Netvibes (www.netvibes.com), Feedly (www.feedly.com), and Newsblur (www.newsblur.com).

Of course, not all sources of information can be aggregated. Social networking sites such as Twitter, Facebook, and Goggle+ allow affinity-based community discussions with individuals, organizations, associations, PLN groups, and news sources (see Figure 10.2 for subscribing to a group on a social network). Teachers can also use real-time interaction tools such as Skype and Google hangout to connect and collaborate with others around the world. For example, Cathy Mere, first discussed in Chapter 9, set up a Google hangout to discuss how to include Google forms in Evernote after finding several teachers on Twitter who were also interested. Real-time conversations are useful for seeking one-on-one support and feedback and for building relationships.

Even with aggregation through RSS feeds and social networking sites, engaging with and monitoring all this information can still overwhelm a teacher. As such, consider starting with one tool, such as Twitter, building a network of trusted people to follow, and expanding to other sources as you become more comfortable accessing and navigating multiple sources of information. Add people and sources to your PLN that provide support, new ideas, teaching techniques, best practices, instructional models, feedback, collaboration opportunities, and conversations. Cull sources that do not. In this way, over time, you will cultivate a PLN that contributes to your professional growth and expertise. The payoff is worth the investment of time.

Internet projects. When teachers become involved in their PLNs, their passion often prompts them to get involved in collaborative projects with local, national, and international colleagues. An Internet project is a collaborative learning experience between two or more classrooms at different locations that takes place over the Internet. These projects can be initiated by individual teachers or coordinated through a website.

Linda Yollis, who teaches a combination 2nd- and 3rd-grade, is one teacher who initiated an Internet project. Her classroom blog (yollisclassblog.blogspot.com.au) has won the Best Class Blog award from Edublog for three consecutive years. In early 2009, Linda came across Kathleen Morris's class blog in Victoria, Australia and left a comment. From this came a rewarding friendship and collaborative adventure, which according to Linda:

has now spanned over 3 years and connected eight different cohorts of students. Through-out this time, the classes have moved from isolated to integrated, irregular to frequent, and from the superficial to rich global collaboration. (The Edublogger, 2012)

See Linda's website for examples of the collaborative projects.

The Internet project Journey North (www.learner.org/jnorth) engages students in a global study of wildlife migration and seasonal change (see Figure 10.3). K–12 students share their own field observations with classmates across North America. They track the coming of spring through the migration patterns of monarch butterflies, bald

Figure 10.1. Examples of PLNs and Tools Available

- Online PLN groups
  - Classroom 2.0 (www.classroom20.com)
  - The Educator's PLN (www.edupln.ning.com)
  - edWeb.net (www.edweb.net)
- Professional associations and organizations
  - ReadWriteThink (www.readwritethink.org/professional-development)
  - English Companion Ning (www.englishcompanion.ning.com)
- Online education news and journals
  - Edutopia (www.edutopia.org)
  - Education news (www.educationnews.org)
- Webinars and webcasts
  - PBS (www.pbslearningmedia.org/)
  - EdWeek (www.edweek.org/ew/marketplace/webinars/webinars.html)
- Podcasts
  - IRA (www.reading.org/general/publications/podcasts.aspx)
  - Infinite thinking (www.infinitethinking.org)
- Blogs
  - Literacy 2.0 (www.literacytwopointzero.blogspot.com)
  - Free Technology for Teachers (www.freetech4teachers.com)
  - Literacy Beat (www.literacybeat.com)
- Video
  - SchoolTube (www.schooltube.com)
  - TeacherTube (www.teachertube.com)
  - Teaching Channel (www.teachingchannel.org)
- Twitter (www.twitter.com)
- Social bookmarking
  - Diigo (www.diigo.com)
  - Delicious (delicious.com)
- Social networking
  - Google+ (plus.google.com)
  - Facebook (www.facebook.com)
  - Real time video chat tools
  - Skype (www.skype.com)
  - Google hangouts (www.google.com/+/learnmore/hangouts)

Figure 10.2. Process of Subscribing to the Social Networking Site Google+

Figure 10.3. Journey North Collaborative Online Projects

eagles, robins, hummingbirds, whooping cranes, and other birds and mammals; the budding of plants; changing sunlight; and other natural events. Examples of other Internet projects are as follows:

- iEarn (collaborate.iearn.org), which fosters critical thinking and research skills, cultural awareness, and community involvement.
- The Flat Stanley Project (www.flatstanley.com), which connects classrooms as students talk about, track, and write about Flat Stanley's journeys and adventures.
- Epals (www.epals.com), which connects students with other students for collaborative projects.

Involve students in creating personal technology-supported projects, such as digital storytelling and biographies, which provide authentic opportunities for students to bring their home culture into the classroom and share with students around the world.

Participation in Internet projects can be extremely rewarding for teachers *and* students. Labbo (2005) states:

It is clear that when students gather and share cultural information for a cross-cultural Internet project, students engage in reading that is inherently meaningful, insightful, and motivating. The Internet opens up the world to students and helps them develop a respect for diversity. (p. 174)

However, collaboration is built on relationships that take an investment of time. The following are a few guidelines:

- Start small, working with a local class before joining a global project.
- Look for classes of a similar age, technology experience, and literacy standards.
- Clearly articulate your shared expectations and goals for the project.
- Set a time frame in which the project will be completed.

SHARING YOUR OWN EXPERIENCES

I am a big proponent of teachers as writers, and social networks such as blogs provide an avenue for teachers' voices to be heard around the world. As teachers build their PLNs, they will find fortitude, camraderie, and inspiration from others who have made the decision to share their teaching lives online. Consider the following blog post from 5th-grade teacher Jennifer Marten (2012):

Evaluate me, please. Just remember my worth shouldn't be determined by some arbitrary value added model based on subpar standardized tests. It should come from what I do with the students I have each year, from my professional growth, and from formative, on-going conversations.

This post was nominated by other educators for the 2012 Most Influential Blog Post awarded by Edublogs. In addition to being nominated for the award, the post has received over 50 comments to date. Jennifer's heartfelt post clearly struck a chord with readers.

As you continue to read and comment on other teacher's social media posts, you may slowly gain the confidence and passion to start your own blog. Twitter, Facebook, and Google+ support quick, brief, ongoing communication and information sharing, but blogging allows for longer, more in-depth posts. There are many other reasons to consider starting a blog. Blogging allows teachers to write for a purpose and audience that matters. Sharing strategies, lessons, reflections, and resources with others who will learn from them just as you have learned from your PLN connections allows you to give back to the profession.

Blogging forces you to analyze your thoughts and actions in a much more methodical way than to simply reflect on your day. It enables you to learn more about your teaching, your students, and the value of your own ideas.

Blogging helps you find your own voice. Every teacher has unique, diverse experiences, skills, and knowledge. Writing will help you to find the power in your own voice as a teacher and share it with others.

Blogging lets you experience the tools of new literacies. By using the same tools your students are using in and outside of school, you are gaining firsthand experience with the skills and strategies they need to compose online in meaningful ways.

Now that you have started thinking about blogging, you might wonder what to blog about. Though you value the varied content on the blogs you read, don't fall into the trap of thinking that your thoughts, reflections, and experiences don't matter. If you are wondering about an aspect of teaching practice or reflecting on reading or a teaching experience, chances are that others are too, and your post may be just what another teacher needs to read. The following are a few considerations:

- Write about what matters to you.
- Write when it is important to you and your professional development, not every day.
- Consider a blogging buddy to collaborate and share writing with (see bookends.booklistonline.com and www.twowritingteachers.wordpress.com).

Finally, let other teachers in your professional circles know about your blog. Teachers are often hesitant to take credit for their accomplishments. Remember, just as you have benefitted from reading other teachers' blogs, other teachers will benefit from reading yours.

Blogging about teaching fosters reflection that is central to good teaching practice. However, it is informal and unsystematic. Teachers can use digital teaching portfolios to document the many aspects of their teaching in a formal and systematic way.

DIGITAL TEACHING PORTFOLIOS

As every teacher knows, the art of teaching is complicated and complex. Teaching portfolios have long been used to document teaching practice, professional growth, and student learning through systematic documentation and reflection. However, the increased demands of accountability and assessment require professional educators to seek new ways of looking at teacher and student information and systematic data collection. Digital portfolios extend the possibilities for documentation and reflection through the use of multimedia, linking, and public feedback.

Multimedia records of teaching practice can include videos of teaching, links to lesson plans, images of student work, audio or videotaped reflections on teaching and student work, and more. The inclusion of multimedia in a teaching portfolio provides a richer picture than static artifacts of what constitutes effective teaching. Digital portfolios also make individual teaching practices public and therefore available for collective learning and knowledge sharing.

The following are a few considerations when creating a digital portfolio:

- *Information overload:* Select just-enough artifacts to exemplify the teaching and learning in your classroom but don't overwhelm the reader. Add an additional resource page for extended examples.

- *Structure and layout:* Make the purpose and content clear and easy to find. Avoid making pages so busy that the reader isn't sure where to look or what to look at.
- *Ease of navigation:* Make navigation easy and institutive.
- *Permission/releases:* Get permission to use student work samples or images, or parent feedback if necessary.

Create portfolios using the same platforms as suggested for students such as blogs, wikis, and websites. Additionally, there are applications specifically for creating a portfolio:

- Portfoliogen (www.portfoliogen.com)
- Dropr (www.dropr.com)
- Pathbrite (www.pathbrite.com)

Figure 10.4 provides an example of a teacher portfolio created using Portfoliogen.

Digital portfolios provide teachers with a way to showcase the teaching expertise and student learning happening in their classrooms every day. They also provide an opportunity for reflection and continued professional growth.

Figure 10.4. Teacher Portfolio Created with Portfoliogen

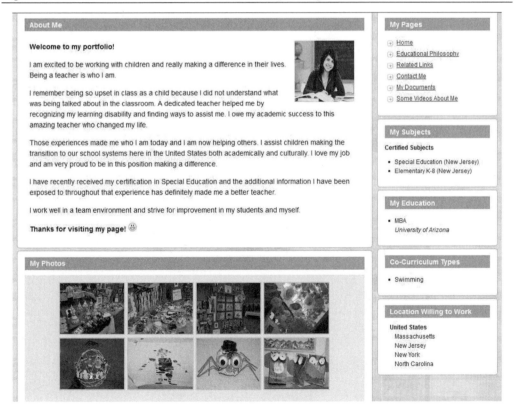

Becoming a part of a PLC and/or curating a PLN, along with the other activities described in this chapter, provides flexible, ongoing, job embedded professional development that can assist teachers with staying abreast of the new literacies of today and beyond. Whether it's literacy 2.0, 3.0, or beyond, staying connected in meaningful ways can assist teachers in preparing to meet the literacy demands of their students now and in the future.

References

Allington, R., & Johnston, P. (2002). *Reading to learn: Lessons from exemplary fourth-grade classrooms*. New York, NY: Guilford Press.

Amazon.com. (2011, January 27). Amazon.com announces fourth quarter sales up 36% to $12.95 billion [Press release]. Available at phx.corporate-ir.net/phoenix. zhtml?c=176060&p=irol-newsArticle&ID=1521090&highlight&ref=tsm_1_tw_kin_ prearn_20110127

Anderson, J. Q., & Rainie, L. (2010, February 19). A review of responses to a tension pair about the impact of the internet on reading, writing, and the rendering of knowledge. Washington, DC: Pew Research Center's Internet & American Life Project. Available at pewinternet.org/Reports/2010/Future-of-the-Internet-IV/Part-2Reading.aspx?r=1

Applegate, K. (2012). *The one and only Ivan*. New York, NY: HarperCollins

Armstrong, A. (2005). *Whittington*. New York, NY: Random House.

Baker, E., Pearson, P. D., & Rozendal, M. (2010). Theoretical perspectives and literacy studies: An exploration of roles and insights. In E. Baker (Ed.), *The new literacies: Multiple perspectives on research and practice* (pp. 1–22). New York, NY: Guilford Press.

Baker, S., Simmons, D. C., & Kame'enui, E. J. (1998). Vocabulary acquisition: Research bases. In D .C. Simmons & E. J. Kame'enui (Eds.), *What reading research tells us about children with diverse learning needs: Bases and basics* (pp. 183–217). Mahwah, NJ: Erlbaum.

Barnwell, Y. (1998). *No mirrors in my nana's house*. San Diego, CA: Harcourt Brace.

Baumann, J., Ware, D., & Edwards, E. (2007). "Bumping into spicy, tasty words that catch your tongue": A formative experiment on vocabulary instruction. *The Reading Teacher, 61*(2), 108–122.

Beck, I., Perfetti, C., & McKeown, M. (1982). Effects of long-term vocabulary instruction on lexical access and reading comprehension. *Journal of Educational Psychology, 74*(4), 506–521.

Beck, I., McKeown, M., & Kucan, L. (2002). *Bringing words to life: Robust vocabulary instruction*. New York, NY: Guilford Press.

Bircher, K. (2012). What makes a good picture book app? *The Horn Book Magazine, 88*(2), 72–78.

Blachowicz, C., Fisher, D., Ogle, D., & Watts-Taffe, S. (2006). Vocabulary: Questions from the classroom. *Reading Research Quarterly, 41*(4), 524–539.

Bomer, R. (1995). *Time for meaning*. Portsmouth, NH: Heinemann.

Boyd, D., & Ellison, N. B. (2007). Social network sites: Definition, history, and scholarship. *Journal of Computer-Mediated Communication, 13*(1), 210–230.

Carmon, P. (2009). *Skeleton creek, book 1*. New York, NY: Scholastic.

Carr, N. (2008, July 1). Is Google making us stupid? What the Internet is doing to our brains. *The Atlantic*. Available at www.theatlantic.com/magazine/archive/2008/07/is-google-making-us-stupid/306868

Carroll, L. (1865). *Alice's adventures in wonderland*. London, UK: Macmillian.

Chall, J., & Jacobs, V. (2003). Poor children's fourth-grade slump. *American Educator. 27*(1). Available at www.aft.org/pubs-reports/american_educator/spring2003/chall.html

Choi, C., & Ho, H. (2002). Exploring new literacies in online peer learning environments. *Reading Online.* Available at www.readingonline.org/newliteracies/lit_index.asp?HREF=choi/index.htm.

Choice Literacy. (Producer). (n.d.). Ralph Fletcher on mentor texts [Audio podcast]. Available at www.choiceliteracy.com/articles-detail-view.php?id=994

Clark, C. (2012). *Children's and young people's reading today. Findings from the 2011 National Literacy Trust's annual survey.* London, UK: National Literacy Trust.

Clark, J., & Paivio, A. (1991). Dual coding theory and education. *Educational Psychology Review, 3*(3), pp. 149–210.

Coiro, J. (2003). Reading comprehension on the Internet: Expanding our understanding of reading comprehension to encompass new literacies. *The Reading Teacher, 56*(6), 458–464.

Coiro, J. (2009). Rethinking online reading assessment. *Educational Leadership, 66*(6), 59–63.

Coiro, J. (2012). Digital literacies: Understanding dispositions toward reading on the Internet. *The Journal of Adolescent and Adult Literacy, 56*(7), 645–648.

Coiro, J., & Dobler, E. (2007). Exploring the online reading comprehension strategies used by sixth-grade skilled readers to search for and locate information on the Internet. *Reading Research Quarterly, 42*(2), 214–257.

Coiro, J., Knobel, M., Lankshear, C., & Leu, D. (2008). *Handbook of research on new literacies.* New York, NY: Routledge.

Crafton, L. (2006). What are communities of practice? Why are they important? *School Talk, 12*(1), 1–2.

Cronin, D. (2003). *Diary of a worm.* New York, NY: HarperCollins.

Cunningham, P. (2008). *Phonics they use: Words for reading and writing.* New York, NY: Pearson.

Cunningham, P., & Allington, R. (2011). *Classrooms that work: They can all read and write* (5th ed.). New York, NY: Pearson.

Cunningham, P., & Cunningham, J. W. (2010). *What really matters in writing: Research-based practices across the elementary curriculum.* New York, NY: Allyn & Bacon.

Cunningham, A., & Stanovich, K. (1997). Early reading acquisition and its relation to reading experience and ability 10 years later. *Developmental Psychology, 33*(6), 934–945.

Dalton, B., & Proctor, C. (2008). The changing landscape of text and comprehension in the age of new literacies. In J. Coiro, M. Knobel, C. Lankshear, & D. Leu (Eds.), *Handbook of research on new literacies* (pp. 297–324). New York, NY: Lawrence Erlbaum.

Dalton, B., & Rose, D. (2008). Scaffolding digital comprehension. In C. C. Block & S. R. Parris (Eds.), *Comprehension instruction: Research-based practices* (2nd ed., pp. 347–361). New York, NY: Guilford Press.

Darling-Hammond, L. (2010). *The flat world and education.* New York, NY: Teachers College Press.

Darling-Hammond, L., Wei, R. C., Andree, A., Richardson, N., & Orphanos, S. (2009). *Professional learning in the learning profession: A status report on teacher development in the United States and abroad.* Palo Alto, CA: School Redesign Network at Stanford University.

Davenport, M. R. (2002). *Miscues not mistakes: Reading Assessment in the Classroom.* Portsmouth, NH: Heinemann.

debf. (2012, October 15). Re. Six ways to use Evernote to capture learning [Blog comment]. Available at reflectandrefine.blogspot.com/2012/09/six-ways-to-use-evernote-to-capture. html?showComment=1350359168866#c3232215687044705284

Digital Book World (2013). Scholastic to publish another transmedia series following success of 39 Clues and Infinity Ring. [Press release]. Available at www.digitalbookworld. com/2013/scholastic-to-publish-another-transmedia-series-following-success-of-39-clues-and-infinity-ring/

Dorn, L., & Soffos, C. (2005). *Teaching for deep comprehension: A reading workshop approach.* Portland, ME: Stenhouse.

Duke, N. K. (2000). 3.6 minutes per day: The scarcity of informational texts in first grade. *Reading Research Quarterly, 35*(2), 202–224.

Duke, N. K., & Pearson, P. D. (2002). Effective practices for developing reading comprehension. In A. E. Farstrup & S. J. Samuels (Eds.), *What research has to say about reading instruction* (3rd ed., pp. 205–242). Newark, DE: International Reading Association.

Edmonds, K., & Bauserman, K. (2006). What teachers can learn about reading motivation through conversations with children. *The Reading Teacher, 59*(5), 414–424.

Edublogger (2012). ISTE 2012: Flattening Classroom Walls with Blogging and Global Collaboration. Available at theedublogger.com/2012/07/02/iste-2012-flattening-classroom-walls-with-blogging-and-global-collaboration/

Enright, E. (1938). *Thimble summer.* New York, NY: Farrar & Rinehart, Inc.

Ferguson, C., Jordan, C., & Baldwin, M. (2010). *Working systemically in action: Engaging family and community.* Austin, TX: Southwest Educational Development Laboratory.

Fisher, P., Blachowicz, C., & Smith, J. (1991). Vocabulary learning in literature discussion groups. In J. Zutell & S. McCormick (Eds.), *Learner factors/teacher factors: Issues in literacy research and instruction* (40th yearbook of the National Reading Conference, pp. 201–209). Chicago, IL: National Reading Conference.

Fleming, C. (2011). *Amelia lost: The life and disappearance of Amelia Earhart.* New York, NY: Random House.

Fleming, D. (1991). *In the tall, tall grass.* New York, NY: Henry Holt and Co.

Fleming, D. (1992). *Lunch.* New York, NY: Henry Holt and Co.

Fleming, D. (1993). *In the small, small pond.* New York, NY: Henry Holt and Co.

Fleming, D. (1997). *Time to sleep.* New York, NY: Henry Holt and Co.

Fleming, D. (2007). *Beetle bop.* New York, NY: Houghton Mifflin.

Fleischman, P. (1988). *Joyful noise: Poems for two voices.* New York, NY: Harper & Row.

Forte, A., & Bruckman, A. (2006). From Wikipedia to the classroom: Exploring online publication and learning. *Proceedings of the Seventh International Conference on Learning Sciences*, pp. 182–188.

Fox, E. (2009). The role of reader characteristics in processing and learning from informational text. *Review of Educational Research, 7*(1), 197–261.

Fox, M. (1983). *Possum magic.* San Diego, CA: Harcourt Brace Jovanovich.

Fox, M. (1986). *Hattie and the fox.* New York, NY: Bradbury Press.

Fox, M. (1988). *Koala Lou.* San Diego, CA: Harcourt Brace Jovanovich.

Fox, M. (1994). *Sophie.* San Diego, CA: Harcourt Brace.

Fox, M. (2000). *Harriet, you'll drive me wild.* San Diego, CA: Harcourt Brace.

Fryer, W. (2010, May 26). Throwing away 6th grade–or–the case for online portfolios [Blog post]. Available at www.speedofcreativity.org/2010/05/26/throwing-away-6th-grade-or-the-case-for-online-portfolios/

Glasgow, J. (1996). It's my turn! Part II: Motivating young readers using CD-ROM storybooks. *Learning and Leading with Technology, 24*(4), 18–22.

Goodrich, H. (1997). Understanding rubrics. *Educational Leadership, 54*(4), 14–17.

Graham, S., & Hebert, M. (2010). Writing to read: Evidence for how writing can improve reading. A Carnegie Corporation Time to Act Report. Washington, DC: Alliance for Excellent Education. Available at www.all4ed.org/files/WritingToRead.pdf

Graham, S., & Perin, D. (2007). Writing next: Effective strategies to improve writing of adolescents in middle and high schools – A report to Carnegie Corporation of New York. Washington, DC: Alliance for Excellent Education. Available at www.all4ed.org/files/WritingNext.pdf

Graves, M., & Watts-Taffe, S. (2002). The place of word consciousness in a research-based vocabulary program. In A. E. Farstrup & S. Samuels (Eds.), *What research has to say about reading instruction* (3rd ed., pp. 140–165). Newark, DE: International Reading Association.

Gray, L., Thomas, N., & Lewis, L. (2010). *Teachers' use of educational technology in U.S. public schools: 2009* (NCES 2010–040). Washington, DC: National Center for Education Statistics, Institute of Education Sciences, U.S. Department of Education.

Green, J. (2005). *Looking for Alaska.* New York, NY: Dutton.

Greenberg, A. (2009). *The 2009 update: Taking the wraps off videoconferencing in the U.S. classroom.* Available at www.wrplatinum.com/Downloads/10122.aspx

Halpern, D., & Hakel, M. (2002). Learning that lasts a lifetime: Teaching for long-term retention and transfer. In D. Halpern & M. Hakel (Eds.), *Applying the science of learning to university and beyond* (pp. 3–7). San Francisco, CA: Jossey-Bass.

Harvey, S. (1998). *Nonfiction matters: Reading, writing, and research in grades 3–8.* York, ME: Stenhouse.

Harvey, S., & Goudvis, A. (2013). Comprehension at the core. *The Reading Teacher, 66*(6), 432–439.

Hattie, J. (2009). *Invisible learning: A synthesis of over 800 meta-analyses relating to achievement.* New York, NY: Routledge.

Henry, L. (2006). SEARCHing for an answer: The critical role of New Literacies while reading on the Internet. *The Reading Teacher, 59*(7), pp. 614–627.

Hicks, T. (2009). *The digital writing workshop.* Portsmouth, NH: Heinemann.

Holt, T. (2010, July 23). Six items in your digital suitcase: opinion [Blog post]. Available at web.me.com/timholt/Intended_Consequenses/Intended_Consequences_v._2.0/Entries/2010/7/23_Six_Items_in_Your_Digital_Suitcase__Opinion.html

Hyerle, D., & Alper, L. (2013). Thinking maps for meetings of the mind. In A. Costa & P. O'Leary (Eds.), *The power of the social brain: Teaching, learning, and interdependent thinking* (pp. 102–114). New York, NY: Teachers College Press.

International Reading Association. (2000). *Excellent reading teachers.* [Position statement]. Newark, DE: Author. Available at www.reading.org/Libraries/Position_Statements_and_Resolutions/ps1041_excellent.sflb.ashx

Ito, M., Heather, H., Bittanti, M., Boyd, D., Herr-Stephenson, B., Lange, P., et al. (2008, November). *Living and learning with new media: Summary of findings from the Digital Youth*

Project. Available at www.macfound.org/media/article_pdfs/DML_ETHNOG_WHITE-PAPER_1.PDF

Ito, M., Horst, H., Antin, J., Finn, M., Law, A., Manion, A., Mitnick, S., Schlossberg, D., & Yardi, S. (2013). *Hanging out, messing around, and geeking out: Kids living and learning with new media.* Cambridge, MA: MIT Press.

Ivey, G., & Johnston, P. (2013). Engagement with young adult literature: Outcomes and processes. *Reading Research Quarterly, 48*(3), pp. 255–275.

Jackson, C. K., & Bruegmann, E. (2009). *Teaching students and teaching each other: The importance of peer learning for teachers* (NBER 15202). Cambridge, MA: National Bureau of Economic Research. Available at www.nber.org/papers/w15202.pdf

Joan Ganz Cooney Center (2012). *Print books vs. e-books.* Available at: www.joanganzcooney-center.org/wp-content/uploads/2012/07/jgcc_ebooks_quickreport.pdf

Johnson, D. (2008). *Teaching literacy in fourth grade.* New York, NY: Guilford Press.

Johnson, S. (2011). *Digital tools for teaching.* Gainesville, FL: Maupin House.

Johnston, P. (2004). *Choice words: How our language affects children's learning.* Portland, ME: Stenhouse.

Jones, T., Brown, C. (2011). Reading engagement: A comparison between e-books and traditional print books in an elementary classroom. *International Journal of Instruction, 4*(2), 5–22.

Kaiser Foundation (2010, January 2010). *Generation M2: Media in the lives of 8-to 18-year-olds.* Available at kaiserfamilyfoundation.files.wordpress.com/2013/04/8010.pdf

Kelm, J. (2005). *Appreciative living: The principles of appreciative inquiry in personal life.* Wake Forest, NC: Venet.

Knobel, M., & Wilber, D. (2009). Let's talk 2.0. *Educational Leadership, 66*(6), 20–24.

Koehler, M., & Mishra, P. (2008). Introducing TPCK. In AACTE Committee on Innovation and Technology (Ed.), *Handbook of technological pedagogical content knowledge (TPCK) for educators* (pp. 3–29). New York, NY: Routledge.

Kymes, A. (2005). Teaching online comprehension strategies using think-alouds. *Journal of Adolescent & Adult Literacy, 48*(8), 492–500.

Kress, G. (2003). *Literacy in the new media age.* New York, NY: Routledge.

Labbo, L. (2005). Fundamental qualities of effective Internet literacy instruction: An exploration of worthwhile classroom practices. In R. Karchmer, M. Mallette, J. Kara-Soteriou, & D. Leu (Eds.), *Innovative approaches to literacy education: Using the Internet to support new literacies* (pp. 165–179). Newark, DE: International Reading Association.

Langer, J., & Close, E. (2001). *Improving literacy understanding through classroom conversation.* Albany, NY: The Center on English Learning & Achievement.

Lankshear, C., & Knobel, M. (2006). *New literacies* (2nd ed.). New York, NY: Open University Press.

Larson, L. (2009). Reader response meets new literacies: Empowering readers in online learning communities. *The Reading Teacher, 62*(8), 638–648.

Leu, D. J. (2006). New literacies, reading research, and the challenges of change: A deictic perspective. In J. V. Hoffman, D. L. Schallert, C. M. Fairbanks, J. Worthy, & B. Maloch (Eds.), *Fifty-fifth yearbook of the National Reading Conference* (pp. 1–20). Oak Creek, WI: National Reading Conference.

Leu, D. J., Leu, D. D., & Coiro, J. (2004). *Teaching with the Internet K–12: New literacies for new times* (4th ed.). Norwood, MA: Christopher-Gordon.

Leu, D., Kinzer, C., Coiro, J., & Cammack, D. (2004). Toward a theory of new literacies emerging from the Internet and other information and communication technologies. In R. B. Ruddell & N. J. Unrau (Eds.), *Theoretical models and processes of reading* (5th ed., pp. 1570–1613). Newark, DE: International Reading Association.

Leu, D., O'Byrne, W., Zawilinski, L., McVerry, J., & Everett-Cacopardo, H. (2009). Expanding the new literacies conversation. *Educational Researcher, 38*(4), 264–269.

Lewis, C. S. (1950). *The lion, the witch, and the wardrobe.* New York, NY: HarperCollins

Lewis, C., & Fabos, B. (2005). Instant messaging, literacies, and social identities. *Reading Research Quarterly, 40*(4), 470–501.

Lin, G. (2011, June 21). Booktalk Tuesday. [Blog post]. Available at www.gracelinblog.com/2011/06/booktalk-tuesday_21.html

London, J. (1903). *Call of the wild.* New York, NY: Macmillian.

Lowry, L. (1989). *Number the stars.* Boston, MA: Houghton Mifflin.

Marten, J. (2012, April 2). Evaluate me, please. [Blog post]. Available at teachfromtheheart.wordpress.com/2012/04/24/evaluate-me-please/

Martinez, M., Roser, N., & Strecker, S. (1999). "I never thought I could be a star": A Reader's Theater ticket to fluency. *The Reading Teacher, 52*(4), 326–334.

Mazer, J. (2013). Associations among teacher communication behaviors, student interest, and engagement: A validity test. *Communication Education, 62*(1), 86–96.

McCarthy, M. (1990). *Vocabulary.* Oxford, UK: Oxford University Press.

McKeon, C. (2010). Reading web-based electronic texts: Using think-alouds to help students begin to understand the process. In B. Moss & D. Lapp (Eds.), *Teaching new literacies in grades 4–6* (pp. 245–257). New York, NY: Guilford Press.

McVerry, J. G., Zawilinski, L., & O'Byrne, W. I. (2009). Navigating the Cs of change. *Educational Leadership, 67*(1). Available at www.ascd.org/publications/educational-leadership/sept09/vol67/num01/Navigating-the-Cs-of-Change.aspx

MetLife Survey of American Teachers: Challenges for school leaders (February, 2013). Available at www.metlife.com/assets/cao/foundation/MetLife-Teacher-Survey-2012.pdf

Mohr, M., & Orr, J. (2009). Reader responsiveness 2.0. *Educational Leadership, 66*(6). Available at www.ascd.org/publications/educational-leadership/mar09/vol66/num06/Reader-Responsiveness-2.0.aspx

Nagy, W. (1988). *Teaching vocabulary to improve reading comprehension.* Urbana, IL: ERIC Clearinghouse on Reading and Communication Skills.

Nagy, W., & Townsend, D. (2012). Words as tools: Learning academic vocabulary as language acquisition. *Reading Research Quarterly, 47*(1), 91–108.

National Center for Education Statistics. (2012). *The nation's report card. Writing 2011: National Assessment of Educational Progress at grades 8 and 12* (NCES 2012–470). Washington, DC: Institute of Education Sciences, U.S. Department of Education. Available at nces.ed.gov/nationsreportcard/pdf/main2011/2012470.pdf

National Center for Literacy Education (March, 2013). *Remodeling literacy learning: Making room for what works.* Available at www.literacyinlearningexchange.org/sites/default/files/ncle_report_final_format_0.pdf

National Council of Teachers of English. (2008). *NCTE framework for 21st century curriculum and assessment* [Position statement]. Available at www.ncte.org/positions/statements/21stcentframework

National Governors Association Center for Best Practices, Council of Chief State School Officers (2010). *Common Core State Standards (English/Language Arts)*. Washington DC: Author.

National Writing Project (with DeVoss, D.N., Eidman-Aadahl, E., & Hicks, T.). (2010). *Because digital writing matters: Improving student writing in online and multimedia environments*. San Francisco, CA: Jossey-Bass.

Nielsen, J. (2006). *F-shaped pattern for reading web content*. Available at www.nngroup.com/articles/f-shaped-pattern-reading-web-content

Nosy Crow. (2013). *The three little pigs* (Version 1.4.4). [Mobile application software]. Available at itunes.apple.com

Oczkus, L. D. (2010). *Reciprocal teaching at work: Powerful strategies and lessons for improving reading comprehension* (2nd ed.). Newark, DE: International Reading Association.

Padak, N., & Rasinski, T. (2008). *Evidence-based instruction in reading: A professional development guide to fluency*. New York, NY: Allyn & Bacon.

Palincsar, A. S., & Brown, A. L. (1984). Reciprocal teaching of comprehension-fostering and comprehension-monitoring activities. *Cognition and Instruction, 1*(2), 117–175.

Palloff, R., & Pratt, K. (2007). *Building online learning communities*. San Francisco, CA: Jossey-Bass.

Parsons, A. (1990). *Amazing spiders*. New York, NY: Knopf.

Pena-Shaff, J., Martin, W., & Gay, G. (2001). An epistemological framework for analyzing student interactions in computer-mediated communication environments. *Journal of Interactive Learning Research, 12*(1), 41–68.

Pew Internet (2013). Trend data (Adults). Available at www.pewinternet.org/Static-Pages/Trend-Data-%28Adults%29.aspx

Phelps, G., & Schilling, S. (2004). Developing measures of content knowledge for teaching reading. *The Elementary School Journal, 105*(1), 31–48.

Piaget, J. (1926). *Language and thought of the child*. New York, NY: Kegan Paul, Trench, and Trubner.

Pinnell, G., Pikulski, J., Wixson, K., Campbell, J., Gough, P., & Beatty, A. (1995). *Listening to children read aloud*. Washington, DC: U.S. Department of Education, Office of Educational Research and Improvement.

Potter, B. (1902). *The tale of Peter Rabbit*. London, UK: Frederick Warne & Co.

Prensky, M. (2001). Digital natives, digital immigrants. *On the Horizon, 9*(5), 1–6.

RAND Study Group (2002). *Reading for understanding: Toward an R&D program in reading comprehension*. Arlington, VA: RAND. Available at www.rand.org/pubs/monograph_reports/2005/MR1465.pdf

Rasinski, T., & Padak, N. (1998). How elementary students referred for compensatory reading instruction perform on school-based measures of word recognition, fluency, and comprehension. *Reading Psychology: An International Quarterly, 19*(4), 185–216.

Ray, K. W. (2004). *About the authors: Writing workshop with our youngest writers*. Portsmouth, NH: Heinemann.

Reader's theater: *A reason to read aloud*. (n.d.). Available at www.educationworld.com/a_curr/profdev/profdev082.shtml

Reeves, T., & Li, Z. (2012). Teachers' technological readiness for online professional development: Evidence from the US e-learning for educators initiative. *Journal of Education for Teaching, 38*(4), 389–406.

Reinking, D. (2001). Multimedia and engaged reading in a digital world. In L. Verhoeven & K. Snow (Eds.), *Literacy and motivation: Reading engagement in individuals and groups* (pp. 195–221). Mahwah, NJ: Lawrence Erlbaum.

Richardson, W. (2010). *Blogs, wikis, podcasts, and other powerful web tools for classrooms.* Thousand Oaks, CA: Corwin.

Richardson, W., & Mancabelli, R. (2011). *Personal learning networks: Using the power of connections to transform education.* Bloomington, IN: Solution Tree.

Riordan, R. (2008). *39 clues: Book 1, The maze of bones.* New York, NY: Scholastic.

Rosenberg, S. (2009). *Say everything: How blogging began, what it's becoming, and why it matters.* New York, NY: Crown.

Rosenblatt, L. (1978). *The reader, the text, the poem: The transactional theory of the literary work.* Carbondale, IL: Southern Illinois University Press.

Ryan, P. (2002). *When Marian sang: The true recital of Marian Anderson.* New York, NY: Scholastic.

Ryan, K., & Cooper, J. (2013). *Those who can, teach* (13th ed.). New York, NY: Cengage.

Schneps, M., Thomson, J., Chen C., Sonnert, G., & Pomplun, M. (2013). E-readers are more effective than paper for some with Dyslexia. *PLoS ONE 8*(9): e75634. Available at www.plosone.org/article/info%3Adoi%2F10.1371%2Fjournal.pone.0075634

Scholastic. (2013). *Scholastic Kids and Family Reading Report* (4th ed.). Available at mediaroom.scholastic.com/kfrr

Schu, J. (2013, April 1). Unplug and read *Bluebird* [Blog post]. Available at mrschureads.blogspot.com/2013/04/unplug-and-read-bluebird.html

Serafini, F. (2012). Reading multimodal texts in the 21st century. *Research in the Schools, 19*(1), pp. 26–32.

Shirky, C. (2010). *Cognitive surplus: Creativity and generosity in a connected age.* New York, NY: Penguin.

Sibberson, F. (Host). (n.d.). Choice Literacy. (Ralph Fletcher on Mentor Texts.) [Audio podcast]. Available atwww.choiceliteracy.com/

Silverman, R., & Hines, S. (2009, May 1). The effects of multimedia-enhanced instruction on the vocabulary of English-language learners and non-English-language learners in prekindergarten through second grade. *Journal of Educational Psychology, 101*(2), 305–314.

Smith, A. (2011, July 11). *Smartphone adoption and usage.* Available at pewinternet.org/Reports/2011/Smartphones.aspx

Sox, A., & Rubinstein-Ávila, E. (2009). WebQuests for English-language learners: Essential elements for design. *Journal of Adolescent & Adult Literacy, 53*(1), 38–48.

Swartz, K. (2013, March 20). 5 tools to help students learn how to learn [Blog post]. Available at blogs.kqed.org/mindshift/2013/03/5-tools-to-help-students-learn-how-to-learn/?utm_source=feedburner&utm_medium=feed&utm_campaign=Feed%3A+kqed%2FnHAK+%28MindShift%29

Swift, J. (1892). *Gulliver's travels.* London, UK: G. Bell.

Sylvester, R., & Greenidge, W. (2009). Digital storytelling: Extending the potential for struggling writers. *The Reading Teacher, 63*(4), 284–295.

Taghdis, S. (1383, Iranian calendar). *How did the moon gain her spot?* Tehran, Iran: Shabaviz Publishing Company.

Thompson, C. (2009, August 24). Clive Thompson on the new literacy. *Wired Magazine, 17*(9). Available at www.wired.com/techbiz/people/magazine/17-09/st_thompson

Time for Kids. (2013). *Hibernating Animals*. Available at www.timeforkids.com/photos-video/video/hibernating-animals-24476

Tschannen-Moran, M., & Johnson, D. (2011). Exploring literacy teachers' self-efficacy beliefs: Potential sources at play. *Teaching and Teacher Education, 27*(4), 751–761.

United States Census Bureau. (2009). *Computer and Internet use*. Available at www.census.gov/hhes/computer/publications/2009.html

Urban, L. (2013). *The center of everything*. New York, NY: Houghton Mifflin.

Valentino, A., & Kantor, M. (2009). *The Amanda project, book 1*. New York, NY: HarperTeen.

Vaughn, S., Martinez, L., Linan-Thompson, S., Reutebuch, C., Carlson, C., & Francis, D. (2009). Enhancing social studies vocabulary and comprehension for seventh-grade English language learners: Findings from two experimental studies. *Journal of Research on Educational Effectiveness, 2*(4), 297–324.

Verhallen, M., Bus, A. G., & de Jong, M. T. (2006). The promise of multimedia stories for kindergarten children at risk. *Journal of Educational Psychology, 98*, 410–419.

Wagner, T. (2008). *The global achievement gap*. New York: Basic Books.

Walters, J., & Bozkurt, N. (2009). The effect of keeping vocabulary notebooks on vocabulary acquisition. *Language Teaching Research, 13*(4), 403–423.

Washburn, K. (2010). *The architecture of learning*. Pelham, AL: Clerestory Press.

Weiser, E., Fehler, B., & Gonzalez, A. (2009). *Engaging audience: Writing in an age of new literacies*. Urbana, IL: National Council of Teachers of English.

Wells, G. (1999). *Dialogic inquiry: Towards a socio-cultural practice and theory of education*. Cambridge, UK: Cambridge University Press.

Wiles, D. (2001). *Love, Ruby Lavender*. San Diego, CA: Harcourt.

Wilhelm, J. (2001). *Improving comprehension with think-aloud strategies*. New York, NY: Scholastic.

Willingham, D. T. (2007, Summer). Critical thinking: Why is it so hard to teach? *American Educator, 32*(2), 8–19.

Wolf, M., & Brazillai, M. (2009). The importance of deep reading. *Educational Leadership, 66*(6), 32–37.

Wood, D. (1998). *How children think and learn* (2nd ed.). Cambridge, MA: Blackwell.

Yolen, J. (n.d.). Interstitial moment. Jane Yolen. Available at janeyolen.com/interstitial-moment-12.

Zanetis, J. (2010). The beginner's guide to interactive virtual field trips. *Learning & Leading with Technology, 37*(6), 20–23.

Index

About the Author

Dr. Denise Johnson is professor of reading education and director of the Literacy Leadership program at the College of William & Mary, Williamsburg, Virginia. She received her Ed.D. in Curriculum and Instruction with an emphasis in Reading from the University of Memphis, Tennessee. She has worked as an elementary classroom teacher, a middle school reading specialist, and a Reading Recovery teacher. She currently teaches graduate and undergraduate courses in reading and language arts methods, and conducts research on literacy, children's literature, and the integration of technology into preservice and inservice education courses and within classrooms.

Dr. Johnson has written several books and articles on literacy, children's literature, and technology, and is active in several professional organizations including serving as chair of the Technology, Communication, and Literacy Committee and serving as president of the Technology in Literacy Education SIG of the International Reading Association. She has conducted numerous presentations and workshops around the country, and continues to work with teachers and children to advance the use of technology in the literacy curriculum.

Dr. Johnson has received the John Chorlton Manning Public School Service Award from the International Reading Association, the Virginia Association of Colleges of Teacher Education's Instructional Leadership Award, and was named the University Professor of Teaching Excellence by the College of William and Mary. She is a National Board Certified Teacher in Literacy: Early-Middle Childhood. Dr. Johnson can be contacted at denise.johnson@wm.edu.